Singular Existence

Leslie Talbot

CITADEL PRESS
Kensington Publishing Corp.
www.kensingtonbooks.com

CITADEL PRESS BOOKS are published by

Kensington Publishing Corp.
850 Third Avenue
New York, NY 10022

All Kensington titles, imprints, and distributed lines are available at special quantity discounts for bulk purchases for sales promotions, premiums, fund-raising, educational, or institutional use. Special book excerpts or customized printings can also be created to fit specific needs. For details, write or phone the office of the Kensington special sales manager: Kensington Publishing Corp., 850 Third Avenue, New York, NY 10022, attn: Special Sales Department; phone 1-800-221-2647.

First printing: January 2007

10 9 8 7 6 5 4 3 2 1

Printed in the United States of America

Library of Congress Control Number: 2006934688

ISBN 0-8065-2799-4

To my Mom and Dad,
who are about to learn a lot more
about me than any of us are ever going to be
comfortable with.

Contents

❊ *Part Three* ❊
A Culture of Strife

❊ *Conclusion* ❊

Introduction:

Waste Not, Want Not

There's a study out there claiming single people are destroying the environment.

According to researchers at Michigan State University, the proliferation of one-person households over the past fifteen years bears a distinct correlation to an alarming depletion of our precious natural resources. Put simply, single people, by nature of our singular existence, are wasteful. We use too much heat, take too many showers, and consume too many Lean Cuisine frozen entrées in microwave-friendly, nondegradable plastic trays. All of this, the study concludes, places you and me on the Ecological Axis of Evil midway between Joe Camel and that drunk guy who totaled the Exxon *Valdez.*

Hello. My name is Leslie, and I am an environmental terrorist.

The media have pounced upon these findings with predictable glee, affording it the breathless "told ya so!" enthusiasm with which it embraces any news item that will most effectively traumatize the 95 million single Americans who are all thrashing around out there wreaking our self-centered swath of ecological carnage across the land.

"But I recycle! I walk to work! *I buy free-range chicken!*" protests Boston bachelor Joseph L. Halloran, thirty-four, upon discovering his 452 square feet of cockroach-infested studio space on Beacon Hill is the epicenter of a global warming juggernaut that will someday decimate the entire universe.

Someone really needs to kidnap Mr. Halloran and leave him locked in the trunk of a Zipcar with a reusable cloth grocery bag over his head until he comes to his senses.

Because *I know*. I know what's really going on here. And, take my word for it, it has nothing to do with the rain forest, or the spotted owl, or the skyrocketing mercury level at the neighborhood fish pier.

This is just the latest salvo in a war of attrition that has been waged against me my entire adult life.

They started with fear—issuing ominous warnings about herpes, AIDS, and the biological time bomb that is my ever-shriveling uterus. They've dabbled in bribery, dangling all sorts of tax breaks and workplace benefits in front of me, mine for the taking if only I relent, marry *someone*, and begin replicating with all due speed. They've lobbed accusations of selfishness and superficiality every which way and made dire predictions of a lifetime of crushing loneliness and bitter regret. And now they've resorted to guilt—the most insidious tactic yet in a vast, intricate conspiracy concocted by political hacks, television moguls, Chick Lit publishers, the Walt Disney Company, and Dr. John Gray to shame me into settling down and reproducing as quickly and prolifically as possible. All so they can peddle *Little Mermaid* videos to my kids, buy my vote with secret tax cuts for parents, brainwash me into a malleable stupor, and sell a bazillion copies of *Mars and Venus Save the Earth* to panic-stricken singles like you and me.

To address the environmental havoc wreaked upon our fair planet by the Nefarious Single Scourge (i.e., me) a motley assortment of self-styled "experts" have joined the crusade and come up with an array of remedial policy recommendations, each more disturbing than the last. One representative from the Massachusetts Green Party offers a particularly odious proposal: *co-housing for singles!* She envisions a "village-like atmosphere for young and old." I envision coming home after a long day at the office, plopping myself down next to the kegger, and having to look at my fifty-six-year-old roommate getting her freak on with her octogenarian boyfriend two couches over while some foul-smelling geriatric frat boy named Bluto vomits his dentures onto my feet after one too many Jell-O shots.

I know, I know. It's all for a good cause. We'd be saving the environment. *For the children.*

I'll tell you what. Here's a counterproposition: When all of my happily married, blissfully procreating friends agree to trade in their Lincoln Navigators for tandem bikes, when they stop supersizing their Happy Meals and start recycling their Pudding Pop sticks, and when they begin laundering their cloth diapers by hand in big wooden tubs with Tom's of Maine Natural Laundry Soap, then I might—*might*—think about getting a roommate.

Until then, folks, I'll be staying right where I am.

Wasting away before your eyes.

Part One

Hopelessly (Out)Dated

Chapter One

Fully Uncommitted

A few years ago, I took a little hiatus from dating.

Part of this was involuntary—the job I had at the time required a great deal of travel, something had to give, and it wasn't like I was going to give up TV or anything, so that something had to be my social life. But, the truth is, it was mostly a conscious choice. After twenty-odd years in the dating world, I have come to understand five basic truths about myself:

Basic Truth #1:
I tend to be strongly attracted to men who are, for the most part, unattainable, unsuitable, or unworthy of my love in one way or another (i.e., they are mean to me and make me sad).

Basic Truth #2:
I do not deserve to be the object of such meanness, nor do I enjoy feeling sad; ergo, I will no longer date these men.

Basic Truth #3:

The majority of men who are attracted to *me* are, for the most part, (a) married; (b) septuagenarians; (c) addicted to one or more mind-altering and usually illegal substance; (d) *mind-numbingly* stupid; (e) unappealing for various other reasons not already noted, most of which are petty and trivial and will make you think I am a terribly shallow person if I told you what they were; (f) all of the above.

Basic Truth #4:

The unappealing men denoted in Basic Truth 3(e) above have, most likely, done nothing to cause me to find them so repugnant. I *am* shallow. I *am* petty. I am not someone who needs to "get to know" someone before she decides whether she likes him. I make up my mind about people immediately, rarely change it, and, on the infrequent occasions I do change it, inevitably realize I was right about the person in the first place and run screaming into the night.

Basic Truth #5:

That's just the way I am. And I know it.

And all this, more than my busy work schedule and irrational devotion to Comcast Digital Cable, was what led to my dating hiatus.

My friends, however, refuse to buy this explanation. They are convinced my aversion to random dating is the adult manifestation of some unacknowledged childhood trauma that has left me so vulnerable and frightened I can't share my heart with anyone for fear of being hurt, and that I therefore avoid any semblance of a committed relationship in order to shield myself from such hurt.

They're half right.

Whether it's the crushing pain of having my heart broken or the crushing guilt I always end up feeling when I know I'm about to break someone else's heart, I don't know. But once I came to the conclusion that I no longer wanted to have my feelings stomped upon by the unworthy, I realized I had no business stomping upon anyone else's feelings, either. The way I see it, my hang-ups are my hang-ups, for better or worse. And I don't think it's right to foist off my neuroses onto someone else simply because he has committed the unforgivable sin of liking me more than I like him. So these days, I prefer to wait to dive into a relationship until someone comes along whom I can be reasonably certain is a nice person, and whom I can be reasonably certain I am attracted to.

> But at this point in my life, I'd willingly trade an entire year of bad first dates for one really good one.

And, yeah, I'm still waiting. But at this point in my life, I'd willingly trade an entire year of bad first dates for one really good one. Although it's hard to say this to people without coming across as sanctimonious, or, even worse, insensitive to their own pain.

All of which was why I found myself at a loss for words when my friend "K" spent a not-so-long-ago Friday evening prostrate on my sofa. She was sobbing her mascara off over yet another guy who had swooped into her life, dizzied her with proclamations of love at first sight, and then swooped off again without so much as a "thank 'ee kindly, ma'am"—only to return three more times over the course of as many months to repeat the cycle over and over again.

"He's just a commitmentphobe!" K sniffed as I passed her a fresh tissue and refilled her wineglass. "He told me he'd had issues with commitment before, but he swore he'd gotten over them! And it's not like I was pressuring him for a relationship—*he* was chasing *me*! What's he so afraid of?"

I didn't have the heart to tell her the truth. He's not afraid of anything. There's no deep psychological Armageddon raging beneath that glossy head of slicked-back hair.

The guy is just a jerk.

It is the height of jerkitude to encourage the attention of someone when the feelings are not reciprocated, particularly when you have an established pattern of inconsiderate dating behavior that repeatedly breaks that person's heart. And blaming it on some type of emotional disorder, e.g., "commitmentphobia," is just a big cop-out. When you string someone along knowing you're going to eventually cut and run, because that's what you always do, you're not a commitmentphobe. You're an asshole.

Sure, commitment is a scary, scary concept. *The rest of my life? Eeek!* It scares me, too. But, honestly, if you're over thirty and you still get cold feet after, say, six weeks, and it happens every time you go out with someone, then you would be well advised to stop dating and get your ass into therapy until you get your head on straight. Don't keep telling yourself it's going to be different "this time." It won't. And you know that.

Does this mean you can't go out with someone for a while and then decide you're not right for each other? Absolutely not. That's what dating is for. Hell, that's what *divorce* is for. But if your little routine repeats itself from relationship to relationship without fail, it's a dead certainty you're never going to get past it on your own, no matter how much you want to believe next time will be "it." It won't be. So 'fess up, face up, and flip off, will you?

Now. To those of you who may have fallen under the sway of one of these loathsome individuals at some point: I feel your pain. Hey, I've been there, too—on both sides of the equation. And I can tell you with confidence that the only thing worse than the stifling panic of being trapped in a relationship with someone you don't want to be with, is the humbling realization that you're the cause of that stifling panic for someone else. Trust me—it's a lot easier on the ego to blame some nonexistent psychological syndrome for that kind of panic than to face the truth: that you're so insignificant in the eyes of someone you've come to love, your feelings don't really come into play at all.

So, because I was too cowardly to give to her face the tough love poor, brokenhearted K so desperately needed, I've decided to just rewrite the conversation so I come out the hero (hey, it's my chapter, after all—if you have a problem with that then write your own damn book):

K: You don't understand. It was the most intense relationship I've ever had. We walked on the beach. We cuddled by the fire! Right on our first date he told me he'd never felt this way about anyone before. So why hasn't he called?

L: Two possible reasons. Either he was lying, or he was lying. Look, I totally believe in love at first sight. It happens. But the typical human response to getting struck by that Big Thunderbolt o'Love is not to blurt it out the first chance you get. Love is scary, painful, and, usually, very humiliating. And admitting you are in love is so traumatic you will probably stutter and stammer and die of embarrassment if it somehow does slip out. Tell the truth—he was slicker than the slickest slickster when he said all those syrupy sweet things to you, wasn't he? I'll bet he didn't miss a syllable. You know why? He's said it all before. And not to you.

K: I don't believe you. We had a connection. I could tell.

L: First of all, turn off that TV and hand over the remote. This is not *The Bachelor.* You did not have a "connection." What you felt was acute physical attraction, which is delightful and quite enjoyable on its own. Given enough time and the right person, it might even have blossomed into true love. The problem is, we have been programmed to believe that in order for this type of attraction to be okay, it must be realized on an emotional level. Let that go. Enjoy it for what it is, but don't make it into anything more. Not yet.

K: But . . . but . . . but . . . we talked until dawn!

L: Has he called?

K: But he cried! He actually CRIED!

L: Has he returned YOUR calls?

Just between you and me, here's a bet: I bet he *will* call her. He'll call her in exactly three months, all flowers and apologies, begging for forgiveness. And here's what I'll be too cowardly to tell her then:

K: He called! He misses me! He wants me back!

L: Of course, he misses you! Why wouldn't he? You are an attractive, intelligent, (usually) emotionally stable person who holds undeniable appeal for someone as spiritually barren as he. You're everything he's not, and he's been sitting around reminiscing about all the great things about you and all the good times you had together. He's probably even convinced himself that he's learned his lesson and can now truly appreciate you. Don't fall for it.

K: You mean he's lying to me? AGAIN?

L: Yes. And, depending on how much of a selfish jerk he is, and how many times he's done this before, he may be lying to himself as well. Maybe he really does believe it will work this time. Maybe he's lonely. Or maybe he knows himself all too well and just doesn't give a rat's ass—he's having an emotional crisis, and the quickest fix he can think of is to snap his fingers and see how many of his exes will come trotting back to him. Regardless, the only person who matters to him in this equation is *him*, and THAT is what he is not telling you. He's lying by omission.

K: But if I'm the one he's reaching out to, doesn't that mean that deep down he must care about me?

L: No. Not really. Because if he really did care about you, he'd realize that your feelings matter more than his immediate needs, and he'd decide that the last thing in the world he should do is cause you any more pain. He'd leave you alone. If he does that, then maybe I'll believe he's worth the risk. If not, well . . . Here.

Have another tissue.

N…

Chapter Two

Just Desserts

I once dumped a guy because he ordered dessert for me on our first date.

Or so my friends would have you believe, citing this date as the harbinger of my downward spiral into a miserable life of solitary unfulfillment and the cold consolation of online crosswords, Soup for One, and Lifetime Television for Women.

I, on the other hand, have a rather different take.

To begin with, I only agreed to the stupid date in a rare moment of weakness. I was harangued into it by my well-meaning (read: married) friends, who convinced me I was intransigent, unreasonable, and that my expectations were hopelessly out of whack with the harsh realities of the dating world.

"Beggars can't be choosers," my tactless friend Cheryl remainded me, as she prodded me into grudgingly accepting an invitation for an evening out with "Joe," a guy I had met at a party the week before.

I knew the date was going to such the instant he put me in charge of picking the restaurant. I so hate it when they do that. It's a trap. If you pick a place that's too fancy you're immediately labeled "high maintenance" and you can bet he'll spend the rest of the date devising clever little tests to see if you're going to be too expensive to take out again. But if you settle on a place that's too low end, you will telegraph a visible lack of self-esteem that will give him license, if he is so inclined, to dump all over you for the remainder of the date or the entire duration of the relationship, whichever lasts longer. Even on the off-chance he is trying to be considerate by asking you to pick the restaurant, he has, in fact, just signaled in blazing red neon that he either hasn't put any time or thought into the date—ergo, why should you—or that he honestly doesn't know where to go because he is a hapless rube who never leaves his apartment except to venture to the neighborhood video store to rent porn. In either case, he is kicking off the date on a gimpy foot of resentment from which it will likely never recover.

That's why I always make it a point to have three "first date" restaurants, cunningly located at strategic points across the city, tucked up my sleeve for just such occasions. Restaurant Number One, in the Financial District, is my restaurant of choice for the "I'm not really sure I like you so let's meet after work for drinks that may or may not turn into dinner" First Date. Restaurant Number Two, conveniently around the corner from my apartment, is my favored spot for the "we really don't have anything in common and we both know it so let's just get drunk and rush through dinner so we can run back to my place" First Date. And Restaurant Number Three, in Boston's trendy South End, is a bit more upscale than the first two and eminently suitable for the "yes, I am a grownup and

I am actually admitting this is a date" Big Time Saturday Night First Date.

All three are studies in neutrality: reasonably priced but by no means cheap; nicely decorated but not too over the top; and well-regarded locally for serving interesting dishes that aren't too exotic—in case he has some bizarre food allergy that could trigger an embarrassing end-of-date trip to the emergency room. Oh, and all three have full bars—a hard and fast requirement for either (a) livening up those less-than-sparkling Awkward First Date conversations; or (b) (see Restaurant Number Two, above).

Since this was an "after work for drinks that may or may not turn into dinner" First Date, we met up in Restaurant Number One, a nice little French-style bistro with an attentive waitstaff and a nice wine list. And drinks did indeed turn into dinner, even though I had concluded immediately upon seeing Joe again that my first instinct had been correct and he wasn't really The One for me. But he insisted on springing for the meal, and I was still chafing under the "arbitrarily picky" label everyone from my best friend to my otherwise-cool boss had slapped on me, so I was determined to stick it out and prove to them all how open minded I could be. Plus I was hungry. And it was by no means an awful time. In fact, I hadn't even gotten around to trotting out the "big day tomorrow, gotta get some sleep" Bad Date Escape Excuse when the waiter arrived to take our dessert order.

I declined the proffered menu and requested a double espresso instead.

"Don't you want dessert?" Joe asked, nudging his own menu toward me.

"No, thanks," I replied, taking a daintier-than-warranted sip of what was left of my wine.

"How come?"

"I'm just not a big dessert person." That's only partially true. Okay, it's a complete lie. I love dessert and would gobble it down for breakfast, lunch, and dinner if I could. But I've gotten into the healthy habit of not ordering it because it's a big waste of calories that could be more enjoyably expended on beer, margaritas, and other tasty alcoholic beverages.

He sat back and gave me what was probably intended to be an admiring once-over (if there is such a thing), but instead made me so uncomfortable I found myself slowly sliding so far down in my seat I thought I could glimpse a wad of congealed gum stuck to the underside of the table. "But you look great!" he said. "You can afford a nice dessert . . . once in a while!"

That was about the time my brain began the slow simmer that marks my emotional transition from bemused annoyance to outright loathing. First, because he immediately attributed my refusal to vanity (which was *technically* accurate, but *still* . . .). Second, who was *he* to decide whether or not I was dessert worthy, let alone give me permission to indulge? It was our first date! You're not allowed to pull that shit until you're cohabitating! And, third, I had already said no. And No Means No. At least that's what they always taught us in those college date rape seminars.

In what I thought was an admirable attempt to remain calm and polite, I picked up my wineglass, drained it, and set it down carefully before replying, "Well, thanks for the compliment, but I'm fine for now. Really."

He picked up the menu and flapped it at me. "How about a piece of cake?" he boomed, attracting the unwelcome attention of the diners at the next three tables. "I'll bet you like chocolate—girls always like chocolate! Look—here's a 'flourless chocolate torte.' That sounds good, doesn't it?"

Not when it's pronounced "tor-TAY" in front of the entire restaurant, it doesn't. But it occurred to me that maybe he really wanted his own dessert but was holding back because he felt funny only ordering for himself. So, mentally congratulating myself on my sensitivity and brilliant powers of compromise, I smiled benevolently and said, "I'll tell you what—if you order something, I'll have a bite, okay?"

He pounced. "See? I *knew* you wanted something! Come on—get one for yourself! *It's okay!*"

I considered reminding him that single people are not required to obtain permission from our dinner companions to order dessert. That is one of the upsides to being single. But I didn't trust myself to say anything other than, "I. Really. Don't. Want. Anything."

One would think my gritted teeth and clenched smile would have clued him in that it was now time to Just Shut Up. But, to paraphrase Forrest Gump—who was beginning to look a hell of a lot more appealing than my date at that point—clueless is as clueless does. And so he just *had* to push it over the edge.

"Aww . . . come on," he simpered, making a revolting smacking sound with his lips. "I'll be *weally, weally sad* if oo don't get something *nummy*." *Smack, smack, smack*.

Oh my God. Oh my God. He was baby talking. He was actually baby talking *me on our first date.* Forget cohabitating—you're not allowed to pull THAT shit until there's an actual BABY in the equation!

I leapt to my feet and shrieked, *"For the love of God, man! Why are you trying so hard to force me to do something I clearly do not want to do?"*

Okay, that's a bit of an exaggeration. I didn't really leap to my feet and shriek that. In fact, I didn't shriek at all. Oh, and I didn't leap to my feet.

Instead, I remained seated, calmly asked him to order me a crème brûlée (which was excellent, by the way—just the exact degree of crispiness on top and nicely warm but not too runny on the inside), ate it slowly while glaring tiny invisible daggers at his head and pointedly refusing to share, and spent the next three weeks ducking his calls.

And *this* is the incident my friends refer to as "the time Leslie dumped a guy because he ordered dessert for her on their first date."

The worst part was, even when I made it clear I never wanted to see him again, he *still* didn't get it. Never mind that I had barely spoken to him for the short remainder of our ill-fated date. Or that when we pulled up to my apartment I hurtled out of the car, house keys at the ready, before he even came to a complete stop. Or that I ran into my building with neither a thank-you nor a backward glance. He just kept leaving these long-winded, chatty messages on my voice mail, which I eventually began deleting without playing back. It was as though he thought that, by sheer dumb will, he could wear me down into going out with him again. Much the way he wore me down into eating the crème brûlée that had been the cause of so much grief in the first place.

He eventually did get the message when we ran into each other in a sporting goods store several weeks after the Night of the Evil Brûlée. Well, he ran into me, that is. I just ran away. Yes, that's right. I looked right into his face and promptly veered left, ducked behind a large rack of half-price running shorts, and watched sadly through a gauzy filter of blue Gore Tex as he exited the store, slumped and dejected, but, I fervently hoped for his sake, a little the wiser for his heartbreak.

Of course, the trio of Singing Chipmunks who comprise my circle of immediate acquaintances all had to weigh in with their opinions on the matter:

Cheryl: You're being ridiculous. You're way too judgmental. Nobody's perfect.

Cathy: Don't come crying to me when you're old and alone. Nobody's perfect.

My Otherwise Cool Boss (for the Man's Perspective): Dude, that's harsh. He was just trying to be nice. Besides, nobody's perfect.

It seemed futile to try to get them to see it from my perspective. It wasn't about perfection, or lack thereof. Nor was it about the poor planning, the less-than-sparkling dinner repartee, the mangled pronunciation of flourless French pastries, or even the baby talk. Not really.

It was about the *disconnect*. That sense of hopelessness you feel when you're trapped in a conversation with someone who *just isn't getting you*. Someone who already has his own idea of who he wants you to be and is so consumed with jamming you into that predetermined mold he is utterly incapable of acknowledging that you're *just not that person*.

When you're in that situation, you have three choices. You can take the path of least resistance, as I did, and pray silently for a speedy end to the evening. Alternatively, you can contort yourself like an agonized pretzel to try to fit that predetermined mold, and then spend the rest of your life fighting that same sense of hopelessness while trying to convince yourself you're really quite comfortable after all. Or, if you believe the outcome is worth influencing, I suppose you can stand on principle, strike a blow for individuality, and eventually—*maybe*—bring the other person around to your way of thinking. But to what end?

Had I held my ground back in that restaurant, I would have simply been investing time and energy trying to fix a relationship I had no interest in continuing in the first place. Instead, I simply projected outward by, say, fifty years, and tried to imagine what it would be like to feel that same frustration and have that same type of argument, again and again, every day, for the rest of my life.

Compared to *that*, I'll take the crème brûlée any day.

Chapter Three

The Rules of Disengagement

Having spent a large portion of my twenties and thirties hiding in ladies' rooms, stairwells, and—on one occasion—a coat-check closet while attempting to avoid unpleasant encounters with ex-dates whose calls I never returned, I am prepared to admit that I am a complete wuss when it comes to breaking up with someone. I can't help it. I hate confrontation because it always makes me cry, even when it's only been like, one date, and the guy really just got on my nerves for something as innocuous as ordering a glass of "white cabernette" at the snooty wine bar I insisted on going to. So I'll do whatever is necessary to avoid an uncomfortable situation, even if it involves cowering behind a large potted plant until the offending party gives up and goes away.

Despite—or perhaps because of—my cowardice as a Dumper, I do consider myself a damn good Dumpee. I'm a good Dumpee because I know how to take an oblique hint and make myself scarce. In fact, sometimes I have been known to take an oblique hint that is so oblique even the hinter doesn't realize it has been given. I'm *just that good*.

Let me tell you—when it comes to dating, I have

learned through two decades of trial, error, and public humiliation that it is always better to err on the side of *not* making a fool of oneself.

Would that everyone followed my example.

But, alas, they don't. Because most of us don't know how to take—let alone give—a hint, oblique or otherwise. There's just way too much stupidity involved. Add to the stupidity the fact that dating invariably brings out the worst in everyone, and suddenly everyone in the world

> I have learned through two decades of trial, error, and public humiliation that it is always better to err on the side of *not* making a fool of oneself.

metamorphoses into a complete asshole. Nice people turn mean. Smart people turn stupid. And stupid people—well, they just become so damn oblivious it's a wonder they can function at all in normal society. And, meanwhile, the rest of us just flail around, trying desperately to make sense of it all, sometimes succeeding, but more often than not screwing it all up even worse than it already was.

The truth is, no one—except for the worst kinds of sadists and this guy Bob I dated for six weeks in 1996— really *wants* to hurt anyone else's feelings. So we rely on hints, half-truths, and, in my own case, poorly executed evasion tactics to do the job for us. Then we sit around, all puzzled and annoyed, complaining about how the Rejected Party "just doesn't get it."

It would be much easier for everyone, I think, if there were a set of rules—a Universal Code of Conduct, if you will—to govern our actions on the front lines of the Dating Wars. A way for us all to arrive at a common understanding as to what is and is not acceptable in the wild and wacky world of romantic rejection. Especially when it comes to breakups.

So, in an attempt to improve the lines of communication down here in the trenches, I hereby present to you a set of breakup guidelines I have dubbed "The Rules of Disengagement." Feel free to take notes in the margins and make multiple copies to distribute to your friends if you are so inclined.

❉ *The Rules of Disengagement* ❉

Part One (for the Dumper)

Since the earliest stages of any courtship are marked not in Real Time but in Date Time (i.e., the number of dates that have occurred over the course of the relationship), the end stages of said courtship must follow suit. This is good news for serial monogamists, who can maneuver through the entire cycle in a single weekend and still have time to catch up on e-mail before Monday morning rolls around; but bad news for multitaskers, who will probably have to import their calendars into an Excel spreadsheet in order to accurately monitor the progression of their various liaisons. In either case, the degree of postdate interaction required to terminate the relationship depends upon the amount of Date Time that has elapsed:

ONE DATE

Free pass. This is your "Get Out of Bed Free" card. After a single date, there is no obligation on your part to either make or return a follow-up phone call, no matter what happened on the date. The "First Date" designation also applies to one-night stands, drunken hookups with soon-to-be-former friends, and instantly regretted nostalgia sex with amorous exes who still carry a flame. It's basically your casual sex catchall category, but if you feel you really do want to see the person again before you decide for sure, you are allowed one phone call. If that phone call is not returned (see "Rules of Disengagement, Part Two, for the Dumpee," page 24), you must *stop calling on the spot*. Do not pass "Go," do not collect one hundred Trojans. You're done.

TWO OR THREE DATES

If no sex has occurred—woo-hoo! Another free pass! You are hereby released from any and all commitments, express or implied. If sex has occurred, however, you are obliged to place one "Conscience Call" to the Rejected Party, a.k.a. the Dumpee, at a number and/or time you know for certain the Rejected Party will not be available. For example, the call may be placed to the Rejected Party's home when the Rejected Party is at work, or vice versa. The goal of the Conscience Call is to leave a vague message which: (a) acknowledges the fact that, yes, you have had sex with this person; but also hints that (b) no, you will not be having sex with this person again.

If the Rejected Party is following his or her own set of guidelines (again, see "Rules of Disengagement, Part Two, for the Dumpee," page 24), the Conscience Call will not be returned and you will both be free to move ahead with your lives, unencumbered by unnecessary guilt, regret, or embarrassment.

FOUR OR FIVE DATES

This is where it starts to get tricky. After the fourth date, you pretty much have to have *some* form of conversation with the Rejected Party. But the rules for this conversation vary depending upon the degree of physical intimacy the couple has entered into. Generally, if you have not had sex with the Rejected Party by the time you want to break up, it's perfectly okay to break up over the phone. But it has to be a *real* conversation and a *real* breakup. No Conscience Calls or oblique hints—just spit it out, hang up as soon as you can, and breathe a deep sigh of relief at your hard-won freedom. If sex has been had, however, there's no getting around it: you have to do it in person (see Six Dates and Up, below).

SIX DATES AND UP

From here on, kiddies, it's the in-person breakup only. Sex or no sex. By the time you get to six dates or more, there's no such thing as a "Get Out of Bed Free" card. The Rejected Party has, by now, invested enough time, money, and/or outfits in the relationship that he or she is entitled to a little face-to-face kiss-off time. Preferably, the in-person breakup is performed in a public venue, the better to avoid a tearful scene and make a hasty getaway. When breaking up in a bar or restaurant, etiquette demands that you pick up the tab before ducking out the back door while pretending to be headed toward the bathroom.

Of course, the best part is, like everything else in life, breakups are reciprocal! You're not in this alone. There are responsibilities on both sides, and, just as there is a code of conduct for the Dumper, there is a corresponding code of conduct for the Dumpee. To wit:

✳ *The Rules of Disengagement:* ✳

Part Two (for the Dumpee)

Sadly, the inconvenient reality of being the Dumpee is that you have little control over your status as such. Like it or not, you are in a reactive mode—and retreat is the only option. Any attempt to regain control over the outcome only serves to make you appear even more foolish and undignified than you already feel and should therefore be avoided at all costs—especially as regards the following:

RE: CONSCIENCE CALLS

Under no circumstances is the Conscience Call to be returned. No exceptions, no excuses. And don't give me the old, "Well, how was I supposed to know it was a Conscience Call?" You know damn well when it's a Conscience Call. No one who really wants to reach you is going to be ringing your office at 9:00 P.M. on a Friday.

RE: EXPLANATIONS

Up to and including the Third Date, you are not permitted to demand an explanation. Accept the sad fact that sometimes things just don't click and move along. Don't go getting everyone uncomfortable by trying to make this whole thing about *you*. It's not about you. It's about the other person. You know, *the person who doesn't like you*. Doesn't being dumped suck enough already? Why on earth would you want to force someone who finds you repulsive to tell you so to your face?

RE: STALKING

There is to be no stalking. No lurking. No "casual" run-ins at, say, the Starbucks in the Dumper's neighborhood. In fact, you and the Dumper are required to give one another a wide berth for at least one month. If you see the Dumper coming around the corner, you are to cross the street and he or she is to change direction immediately so as to avoid mutual discomfort.

RE: THE DRINK AND DIAL

You are not permitted to Drink and Dial unless you have had more than five dates. If you have had more than five dates, you are permitted three Drink and Dials over the course of three months at one-month intervals, if and only if there has been intercourse. If you have not had intercourse, but have had either oral sex or less than five dates, you may Drink and Dial exactly once.*

Effective communication is key to a successful disengagement. Remember, people, subtle hints and vague excuses are virtually useless in navigating a tricky breakup, particularly if the Rejected Party is particularly smitten or inexcusably clueless. When ending a relationship, *what* you say is far more important than how you say it, so, if

---

* And please. No hang-up calls—ever. We all have caller ID. We know it's you.

at all possible—be blunt! Be forthright! Be clear! The Rejected Party will thank you for your refreshing honesty. Someday. Should you, however, find yourself unable or unwilling to adopt the direct approach, you would be well advised to master the basic principles of DumpSpeak: the Vernacular of Euphemistic Cowardice for the spineless masses.

☀ *DumpSpeak* ☀

A Primer (for both parties)

Many of the most unfortunate mishaps and awkward confrontations of our romantic lives could have been avoided entirely, had we only been better versed in DumpSpeak. Please note that these guidelines apply to both Dumpers and Dumpees—since much of the embarrassment surrounding breakups is a direct result of Dumpee cluelessness, it is as important to understand DumpSpeak is it is to speak it.

THE WORK EXCUSE

"I'm really busy at work these days" is DumpSpeak for "I don't ever want to talk to you or see your face again. Go away." Learn this and spare everyone the cruelty of the blunt dismissal or the humiliation of having to have it spelled out for you in front of others.

THE RULE OF UNINTENDED CONSEQUENCES

The phrase "I'll call you" is not to be uttered unless you really intend to follow through with an actual phone call.

So choose your words wisely—the moment you say it, you have automatically committed yourself to at least one more date. Similarly (yes, Dumpees, I mean you), phone calls are not to be demanded, as in "Call me!" Demanding a phone call overrides the "must call" rule and it serves you right for asking.

THE HALL OF FAME

"It's not you, it's me" is to be permanently retired from the Dumping Vernacular. It's been said way too many times, and everybody knows it's a lie.

Penalties for violating the Rules of Disengagement are swift and severe. While a first-time violation will merit no more than a collective eye roll and look of scorn, a second violation results in a one-month suspension of one's Dating License. And if you violate the rules three times (and you people all know who you are . . . *Bob*), you are to be banned from dating for the rest of your life, or as long as you are still physically capable of having sex, which ever comes last.

> "It's not you, it's me" is to be permanently retired from the Dumping Vernacular. It's been said way too many times, and everybody knows it's a lie.

That's three strikes, baby. Three strikes and you're out of circulation. Permanently.

So there you have it. Clean, straightforward, and easy to follow, no? Just think how many awkward misunderstandings and embarrassing scenes could have been avoided if only you'd been carrying these little rules around on a laminated card in your wallet!

Now that you know how to get rid of the people you don't like, the next step is to figure out how to hang onto the ones you do. If we could only put together some guidelines for *that* one, all our problems would be solved.

Never fear. I'm on it.

Chapter Four

Shallow, Self-Centered, and Opinionated Seeks Opposite

In keeping with my mission to bring a sense of order and responsibility to romance everywhere, I have taken it upon myself to launch an undercover investigation into the sordid underbelly of the Online Dating World.

I admit, I embarked on this project with something of a bias. After all, I mean—really—why would you want to date someone you've only met online? Don't you people watch Lifetime Television for Women? Two words: *Stranger Danger!* And, while I do have several very nice Internet friends, I can probably count on the fingers of my mouse-hand the ones I'd actually want to meet in real life. Internet friendships are sustained by one thing and one thing only: guaranteed anonymity! Trust me—a warm, fulfilling relationship is highly unlikely to spring from a keyboard too encrusted with Diet Coke residue and stale Ring Ding crumbs to even tap out a coherent sentence.

Nevertheless, since the Online Personal Ad seems to be the wave of our collective dating future, I felt it my obligation to undertake this task on behalf of all those too fearful to try it for themselves:

❋ *The Recon* ❋

Any spy worth her salt knows the value of good reconnaissance, so the first step in my investigation was a high-level surveil of the terrain before me. Which venue should I choose for my operation? In the interest of authenticity, I wanted to give my potential suitors a fair shot, so I felt it only right that I choose a site as reflective of my lifestyle as possible.

Match.com? Too commercial. eHarmony.com? Too wholesome. Date.com? Too mean. Yahoo! Personals? Too many bad spellers. eDate? Too annoying a font on the home page.

Hmph.

After ruling out most of the big commercial dating sites, I finally selected the space at Salon.com for my little experiment—from what I could see, at least the posters there had a passing familiarity with commas and a spell-checker—and sat down to compose my profile.

❋ *The Cover Story* ❋

Concocting my cover identity (a.k.a. completing the Intrusively Personal Online Compatibility Questionnaire) proved to be far more difficult than I had expected. Not because I'm reluctant to talk about myself—I mean, really, an entire section of the Internet devoted to *me*? What could be better?

No, it was tough because I couldn't imagine even discussing any of these topics with a potential mate, let alone judging anyone based on his responses. But, apparently, would-be Internet daters are altogether comfortable sharing their best-loved onscreen sex scenes with the entire online world, so I muddled through as best I could, and, after a few thousand drafts, I pronounced my work complete and took one final look at the magical prose on the screen before me.

SHALLOW, SELF-CENTERED, AND OPINIONATED SEEKS OPPOSITE

ABOUT ME:

Physical Description: *Since everybody lies on this part anyway, I'm just going to skip it. Trust me. I'm lovely. No, I will not post a photo and set myself up as bait for some demented serial killer. If you're looking for someone to stalk and torture, allow me to direct your attention to the ad below mine: 38-Year-Old Cinderella Seeks Her Prince. She has a photo and seems like she'd be much more your type. Now, skedaddle!*

Star Sign: *Where the hell am I, Studio 54? Do people still really want to know this? I'm skipping this part, too, and if that bothers you, Tony Manero, then you and your white polyester suit can just hop the first subway back to Brooklyn and stay there until hair wings and the BeeGees make their comeback.*

Last Great Book I Read: *War and Peace, by Leo Tolstoy. Oh. You mean a Great Book that I actually* read*? As opposed to, say, buying it to impress the clerks at the Harvard Bookstore and then promptly sticking it in the back of my bookcase to make room for all of the DVD boxed sets of TV shows I keep accumulating? Hmmm. That's different. I'll have to get back to you on that one.*

Most Humbling Moment: *Are you high? I'm supposed to be trying to impress potential mates, not frighten them off! Thanks very much, but I think my* most humbling moment is best kept between the arresting officer and myself. And, believe me, I don't want to hear about your most humbling moment, either. If you and I hit it off, I figure we have about six weeks of sheer, unmitigated bliss ahead of us before the chinks in your shiny white armor start to show. Those six weeks are the best part of the relationship, for God's sake! That's when I'll actually believe you are beautiful and perfect! So, please, I beg you—don't take that away from me by telling me right up front about the time you got your tongue stuck to the flagpole, because if you do then you can just forget about sticking that tongue anywhere in my vicinity. That will be the only image I will ever be able to carry around in my head of you. Forever. In fact, I'll probably end up making up a nasty nickname for you, like Sticky-Tongue Guy, by which all my friends and I will refer to you behind your back while laughing derisively long after your six-week window has slammed shut. You keep your embarrassing secrets to yourself, and I'll do the same. We'll grow disillusioned with one another soon enough, so let's just enjoy the moment, shall we?

Celebrity I Resemble Most: *Nicole Kidman.*

Best/Worst Lie I've Ever Told: *See "Celebrity I Resemble Most," above. Although, to be fair, right after I colored my hair red for the first time, some guy in a bar did tell me I look like Nicole Kidman. Of course, he was hitting on me at the time. Also, he was quite drunk. But since any type of dating interaction you and I have will likely be supplemented by large quantities of alcohol, I think that should count. Besides, Nicole Kidman sounds a great deal more appealing than the celebrity I really resemble: the actress who played Marsha Owens on the old TV show* Mr. Belvedere *("Who?" you ask. "Exactly!" I reply).*

In My Bedroom You'll Find: *A giant closet containing three gas furnaces, one hundred-gallon hot water heater, four electric meters, and the cable wiring for my entire building (never live on the bottom floor of an old brownstone unless you're seeking a close, personal relationship with every plumber,* electrician, and meter-reader in the city); and a deep scratch in my shiny hardwood floor courtesy of an incompetent Boston Water and Sewer contractor who was supposed to be replacing a water pipe but instead managed to gouge up my wall and floor and still hasn't reimbursed me for the damage even though I've called and written to them for over a year . . . oh. Hi. Sorry, I forgot you were there. Now, what was it we were talking about?

What I'd Rather Be Doing Right Now: *Honestly, I can't imagine anything more entertaining than trolling the Internet looking for a boyfriend, can you?*

Why You Should Get to Know Me: *I'm low maintenance! I am so low maintenance I will never make you do any of those Dumb Relationship Things you feel as though you have to pretend to enjoy because you think chicks dig it. This chick doesn't. In fact, if you and I hook up, you are hereby absolved of any and all obligation to perform any and all of the following activities:*

Go for long, romantic walks on the beach: *I find nothing romantic about trudging through mounds of wet sand with the wind blasting in my face, making my mascara run, and ruining my hairdo. What say, we take in a few cocktails poolside instead?*

Have intensely personal postcoital discussions in the dead of night: *Stop babbling and let me sleep, will you?* Yes, *it was good for me, too. Now shut up and close your eyes.*

Cuddle by the fire: *Look, I like my personal space, buddy, so just slide your ass over to your own side of the couch and stay there, okay? And don't even think about spooning me in the middle of the night unless you fancy waking up sprawled out on the floor, bleeding to death from massive head injuries. I need my rest. Otherwise I might get cranky.*

Dine by candlelight: *Well, that one's okay, I suppose, as long as you have decent table manners, it's a nice restaurant, and you're paying.*

ABOUT YOU: Still interested? I thought so! You may go ahead and respond to my ad. Include a link to your own profile and don't forget the photo (hypocrite, shmypocrite! Besides, I'm sure *I'm* not a serial killer. Pretty sure.) Oh, and if you want to maximize your chances of getting a favorable response from me, I'd advise very strongly against committing any of the following Personal Ad Photo Faux Pas:

Posing while hugging your dog: *Let's just say I'm more of a cat person, all right? The last guy I dated who I really liked got a puppy six weeks into our relationship. I never heard from him again. And I'm not sure I want to know why.*

Getting a photo snapped while doing something "rugged" or "outdoors": *Okay, you're fit. I get it. Save your hobbies for your profile. Otherwise you just look like you're trying too hard, and that makes me feel very, very sad for you. Not a promising start to any courtship, particularly an anonymous Internet one.*

Wearing a baseball cap or a hat of any sort, really: *Don't try to hide it—you're bald. That's okay. A receding hairline can be quite appealing, really. Of course, if you look good naked that would certainly help things along.*

Using a professional headshot instead of an ordinary photo: *Unless you are a famous actor (in which case I probably wouldn't want to date you, because, honestly, why would I want to go out with someone even more vain than I am?) this is just a foolish idea. If you have to go out and pay three hundred dollars for a black-and-white still profile of yourself gazing pensively out toward the rolling sea, you're obviously trying to conceal the hideously deformed side of your face that's turned away from the camera. So pack it up, Elephant Man—you're not fooling me.*

Using a Dilbert cartoon instead of a head shot or an ordinary photo: *Admit it—you're an unemployed software engineer whose job was outsourced to Bangladesh three years ago and you're living off of what's left of your 401K while desperately praying for a return to the nineties. Which means I've already dated you.*

Perfect!

Eminently satisfied with the results, I congratulated myself on my wit and compassion, clicked "Send," and completed the exercise by setting up a dedicated e-mail account to capture the flood of replies that were certain to follow.

❊ *Mission Accomplished!* ❊

I received my first response in less than twenty-four hours . . . from an unemployed software engineer whose job had been outsourced to Bangladesh and who obviously had serious reading comprehension problems on top of emotional issues too numerous to detail here. His e-mail—which was actually a six-page love letter/suicide note—closed with the line, "I don't even know why I feel like I can open up to you like this . . . I guess it's because it's a lonely, rainy Sunday morning and your personal ad is the only thing keeping my head out of the oven."

I'm not sure what makes me a worse human being: the fact that I actually felt flattered by his intensity, or the fact that I looked up his photo online, winced, and deleted his e-mail without responding.

Then, after only the briefest hesitation, I deleted my personal ad, too.

Chapter Five

Share and Share Alone

I'm one of those people who are prone to "oversharing." Not in the "spill your guts and pour your heart out to strangers" kind of way, but more in the "this is how I feel; what do you mean you're offended by it?" kind of way. This is probably one reason I've had so many jobs. Tact, diplomacy, and sensitivity are not among my strong suits.

The one area in which I don't overshare is in my personal relationships, which should be, arguably, the area in which we all do our share of sharing. Not only do I not overshare, I don't share. Period. And I kind of prefer that others not share too much, either. Until I get to know you well enough to decide whether I am interested in whatever it is you wish to share, I keep my deepest personal feelings to myself, thank you very much, and invite you to do the same.

This does not sit well with those who, driven by our pervasive societal imperative to establish an instant "connection" with whomever they meet, give no thought to laying out their most intimate thoughts and personal feelings after only a few minutes of conversation. As if, by exposing their deepest psychological traumas, they are somehow binding themselves to you, *daring* you to reject them after all they have shared. Either that, or they're so desperate for human companionship that they overreach, believing even a false connection may be better than none at all. In either case, however, I regard premature vulnerability as the most insidious type of emotional manipulation and reward anyone who engages in it with a first-class ticket on the next flight to Dumpsville.

I don't know what it is about me, but, wherever I am, I tend to be a magnet for the helpless, the bewildered, and the generally clueless. This goes for confused tourists seeking directions to Cheers, Fenway Park, or the Boston Public Garden, as well as for emotionally fragile oversharers, with whom I have spent many a date mired in personal conversations so painful they make me want to crawl under the table and die of embarrassment for both of us.

> I regard premature vulnerability as the most insidious type of emotional manipulation and reward anyone who engages in it with a first-class ticket on the next flight to Dumpsville.

I once went out to dinner with a seemingly normal man who had been separated from his wife for a little over a year. One would think that, given the amount of time that had elapsed since his official separation, he would have gained enough perspective to understand that crying—even the tiniest of sniffly public crying—during the predinner cocktail might frighten off even the most emotionally supportive companion. But, instead, he seemed to regard his little breakdown as a bonding experience, and, upon finally tracking me down at work three weeks after he sent me screaming into the night, demanded to know how I could be so cold and heartless after "allowing him" to "open up to me" the way he did.

We need to get back to the days when dates were fun. When we could go out, enjoy a nice evening and a bottle of wine with someone whose company we appreciate, and not have out to feel like we're auditioning for a guest spot on *Oprah*. Instead, it seems, dating today is either an exercise in oversharing or a study in avoidance. The stakes are so high, the pressure so intense, too many people skip the preliminaries and launch into intimacy without stopping to wonder whether this is really the person they want to entrust with their closest personal secrets.

In an effort to protect my own privacy, as well as that of people who might be inclined to confide a little too much too soon, I employ a five-point strategy to navigating the boundaries of boundary-breaking. These guidelines have not only served me well in guarding my own privacy, but have deflected many a potentially awkward postdate situation such as the one referenced above.

❊ *Boundary Violation #1* ❊

The Childhood Trauma Revisited

AVOIDANCE TACTIC: THE DIVERSION

First dates can be so stressful that even the most banal topic of conversation may trigger the unexpected surfacing of a hitherto-repressed childhood memory so traumatic your date will be reduced to a whimpering, quivering wreck, even as you sit clutching your cocktail, stunned, open mouthed, and at a loss for words. So think fast! Shift the focus of the conversation to a far more horrifying variation of his story to divert his attention from his own emotional pain. For example, let's say your casual reference to a recent heat wave inspires your date to blurt out the gory details of the summer when the fourth grade class bully held his head under water so long he nearly drowned and the paramedics had to be called. Rather than express the concern or sympathy he so obviously craves, simply open your eyes wide and cry, "That reminds me! Did you hear the news story about the girl in Topeka who got sucked underwater when her hair got stuck in a pool drain? They had to send scuba divers down with scissors and a razor in order to rescue her!" That will teach him to moan about his own silly little life—there's a bald girl in Topeka with bigger problems than his!

❊ *Boundary Violation #2* ❊

The Shameful Family Secret

AVOIDANCE TACTIC: THE FAKE-OUT

Family is a tricky subject on many a first date, but it's one that's bound to come up sooner or later, so you'd best be prepared with some preplanned talking points. Depending on how old your date is, you might not want to ask about his parents right away. You never know. Distant relatives are usually a safer bet, conversationally speaking, but in the event your date uses any discussion about family as a pretext to complain about all the therapy bills he has racked up over the years as a result of having to sit on Crazy Old Uncle Bert's lap at family gatherings, throw him off balance with a well-timed Fake-Out. Immediately shift the conversation back to your own family, relating a series of increasingly bizarre but totally innocuous anecdotes about all those wonderful Thanksgivings you spent plucking turkeys at Grandma's farm in the Big Woods of Wisconsin. Note: It doesn't matter whether your grandmother lived on a turkey farm in Wisconsin or in a golf community in Scottsdale. You're never going to see this guy again, so be creative!

✳ *Boundary Violation #3* ✳

The Off-Limits Overreach

AVOIDANCE TACTIC: THE HASTY RETREAT (AS IN "BEAT ONE")

Just because most reasonable human beings consider certain topics completely off-limits during a first date, this doesn't mean your date is following the Reality Playbook. In his mind, religion, sex, and especially politics are all fair game, and no matter how many polite hints and diversionary tactics you employ, he is clearly a man on a mission who will not rest until he either seduces, converts, or enlists you in his cause. Zealots like this cannot be distracted, nor can they be appeased without complete and total capitulation. Forget James Carville and Mary Matalin—love and political differences cannot coexist. Run for your life and don't look back—except to make sure he's not following you.

❊ *Boundary Violation #4* ❊

The Open Wound

AVOIDANCE TACTIC: THE NON SEQUITUR

Everyone has had something bad happen to them at some point in their lives, and some of us bounce back more readily than others. Divorces, custody battles, recent breakups, and sudden job losses leave festering blisters that can burst open and ooze angst at the merest hint of empathy, so be on your guard. No matter how weak and helpless your companion may appear, the moment you succumb to pity and display even a smidgen of sympathy, he will latch onto you like a pit bull on a poodle and you'll never be able to shake him loose. So if you want to avoid an endless stream of complaints about the injustice meted out in Family Court or the inherent unfairness of the modern-day workplace, have a series of well-planned non sequiturs up your sleeve to volley back at him. When he moans about being passed over for a promotion because of those "damn feminists" in the Human Resources department, look him squarely in the eye, smile brightly, and say, "I prefer the Gingerbread Lattè over the Caramel Mochaccino. What about you?" And when he tears up while discussing the intense and bitter wrangling with his former girlfriend over who got to keep the Weber grill, stare idly off into space and remark, "You know, I never realized the word 'pomegranate' only has one *m* in it." Eventually, as any good tennis player will attest, your opponent will grow so confused and exhausted trying to keep up with your unpredictable returns he will collapse under the power of his own serves and end up prone on the court, limp and twitching. Game, set, and match: You.

❊ *Boundary Violation #5* ❊

The Ex Files

AVOIDANCE TACTIC: THE ONE-UPPER

Everyone knows that on the first date, ex-spouses, boyfriends, or girlfriends should only be mentioned in passing, if at all. Typically, the moment the subject comes up you're headed down the road to disaster. And yet, there are those who can't wait to dig in and dish up the dirt, no matter how much it makes their date squirm in discomfort—if there's a bad breakup in his past, he'll be sure to give you the blow-by-blow whether you want to hear it or not. The only thing guaranteed to scare off a date with serious ex issues is demonstrating your own ex issues far surpass his. His ex cheated on him with the golf pro? Your ex cheated on you with Annika Sorenstam. His ex was a raging alcoholic with bipolar tendencies? Your ex was a serial killer. His ex cut up his clothes and burned the house down? Your ex stole top-secret biological weapons from the United States military, used them against thousands of innocent civilians in a remote village just south of Nepal, and covered up his crime with the help of the CIA, the NSA, and Osama bin Laden. That ought to shut the bastard up.

The idea of love at first sight is a worthy cultural ideal. And I do believe in it—to an extent. You can be strongly attracted to someone the moment you meet him or her. You can even have an intuitive feeling that this one is going to be Special.

But the thing to bear in mind is, just because you feel this way doesn't necessarily mean the other person does as well. People take longer to percolate sometimes, and you can't possibly have a meaningful connection with someone within the space of one, two, or even three dates.

And if you think you do, that can only mean one of two things:

He's faking it.

Or, even worse—you're the one who's sharing too much.

Chapter Six

It's Not the Heat . . .
It's the Hostility

Once upon a time, I was asked out on a date by the Nicest Guy in the World.

Well, that is to say, everyone else thought he was the Nicest Guy in the World. I knew him slightly as well, and, although I, too, considered him, if not *the Nicest* Guy in the World certainly *one of the Nicest* Guys in the World, I had not a smidge of interest in dating him. You see, despite being one of the Nicest Guys in the World, he was also one of the Most Unattractive (to me, anyway) Guys in the World.

So I declined his offer, kindly but firmly, telling him I didn't think we should attempt a relationship because we had friends in common and if things didn't work out it might get awkward.

One would think the Nicest Guy in the World would have had at least a passing familiarity with the concept of the polite brush-off and, being the Nicest Guy in the World, graciously accepted my refusal and moved along.

Instead, rather than take the rejection at face value and realize that, when women turn men down for dates it is not because we are *playing* hard to get, it's that we *are* hard to get, the Nicest Guy in the World took it as a topic for Socratic debate. And, during the course of this debate—in which he spent over half an hour attempting to argue me into going out with him—he somehow morphed from the Nicest Guy in the World to . . . well, numerous other personae.

"Are you going out with anyone now?" demanded the Most Increasingly Agitated Guy in the World.

"No."

"Are you interested in anyone now?"

"Not particularly."

"So what's your problem?"

"I'm just not interested in dating right now, period."

"Why not?"

"Because I'm very busy and I don't have a lot of time to devote to a relationship."

"Have you ever even BEEN in a relationship?"

"Yes."

"Well, what happened?" He was actually sweating by now, and his voice had risen three octaves.

"I'd really rather not discuss it, thanks."

"So something DID happen!" crowed the Most Increasingly Agitated Sweaty High-Pitched Voiced Triumphant Guy in the World.

"Like I said, I'd just rather not discuss it."

The Suddenly Angriest Guy in the World slammed his drink down on the table, causing me to jump. "Well, you obviously have a hard time opening up to people, whatever your problem is. So, what, are you going to just stay bitter your entire life?"

"I'm not bitter, and I don't have a hard time opening up to people. I just don't open up to people at random. Now can we please let this go?"

But he had no intention of letting it go. Ever. He stormed off in a huff, got extremely drunk, left the bar we were in, and then slipped and fell down in the snow right outside the front window, thus affirming my original inclination that he wasn't someone I'd be interested in being seen out in public with anyway.

The Angriest Clumsy Drunk in the World remained just that for the next three years, glowering at me from the other end of his beer bottle whenever we ended up at the same party, as if trying to put the lie to my contention that avoiding a relationship would forestall any potential social awkwardness between us. It was plenty awkward, especially when he took to griping to mutual friends that it was obvious he was just "too nice" for someone like me, who was psychologically unable to connect with anyone willing to treat me well. Oh, and he also referred to me as "that bitch." A lot. Eventually, he moved to the Midwest, where the women are rumored to be "not bitches," and, to the best of my knowledge, he remains single and miserable to this very day.

I guess if the (*Not*) Nicest Guy in the World wanted to believe I wasn't interested in him because of the "nice" rather than "unattractive" aspect of his social persona, it was his prerogative. Even if he was stretching the truth a teensy bit. Yes, I have certainly dated and dumped my share of so-called "nice guys" in my day. And, I'll admit, I've pulled the trigger on one or two of them a little too quickly and lived to regret it later (usually upon running into one of my rejects with his new girlfriend a few months after the fact and realizing that that little patch of eczema on his nose is actually kind of endearing in the proper lighting conditions). But I honestly cannot think of a single instance in which I turned down a date with someone simply because he came across as "too nice." Trust me. There was always something else going on there. Maybe he was too whiny. Maybe he got too familiar, too fast. Maybe he had a big piece of chive stuck between his teeth that he couldn't dislodge no matter how hard he tried to suck it off with his tongue without my noticing. But, hey,

> No one wants to acknowledge the real truth: that there is someone out there *who just doesn't like you.*

if someone wants to make himself feel better by telling himself I'm not returning his six-dozenth phone call because he's "just too nice," then who am I to quibble? I'm sure that I myself have been discarded for reasons far crueler and more arbitrary than I care to imagine, so have at it, guys. I'm not going to stop you.

No one wants to acknowledge the real truth: that there is someone out there *who just doesn't like you.* It's much easier to turn the negative into a positive and embrace your rejection as a testament to your own virtue. Why *not* go about your life believing I wouldn't go out with you because you held a door open for me one too many times? It's a hell of a lot more reassuring than finding out it was really because I just couldn't get past that odd wheezing noise you make whenever you try to breathe through your nose.

Not that *I'd* ever be that shallow of course. Not me.

Where people go off the rails, however, is when they begin using these self-affirming little fantasies for sweepingly bitter generalizations about the opposite sex, and then allow those generalizations to inform every measure of their behavior in the dating arena. That's when they start to despise the people they are trying to attract.

The common denominator underlying every unsuccessful date is a general disdain for, well, dating. Just about everyone who dates hates dating. Everyone who doesn't date hates dating—that's why they don't date. The only people who actually enjoy dating are people who shouldn't be dating in the first place: married people, Big Fat Assholes, and a certain individual named Bob I dated for six weeks in 1996.

> **The common denominator underlying every unsuccessful date is a general disdain for, well, dating.**

Maybe it's the fear of rejection, or a resentment of the vulnerability that invariably accompanies the dating experience, but it's quite obvious that there are a lot of people out there in the dating world who would rather not be there and don't mind telling you so. Repeatedly. While trying to date you. Which generates an unfortunate byproduct of our universal loathing of the dating process: a universal loathing of those we are trying to date, accompanied by a radical personality transformation that morphs even the most mild-mannered among us—even the Nicest Guys in the World—into belligerent cretins.

Go to any speed-dating event in this country and you'll see exactly what I'm talking about. *Nobody* is having fun—they're too busy sneering at the "desperate," "fat," "ugly," "superficial," and "loser" fellow speed-daters to enjoy themselves. Not to mention the mortified outrage they might feel when one of those "losers" has the temerity to ask for their number—or even worse, turn them down when *they're* the one doing the asking.

It seems to me that, instead of being so angry with each other, we should be united against the forces that demand we couple up in the first place. Maybe if everyone weren't so intent on proving we're not losers simply because we haven't found The One yet, we'd actually enjoy the process of looking a little bit more. We might find ways to appreciate one another's company without the pressure of

> It seems to me that, instead of being so angry with each other, we should be united against the forces that demand we couple up in the first place.

trying to make something more out of it. And we might even manage to have an honest conversation with a member of the opposite sex that didn't involve debates, arguments, silly "play hard-to-get" rules, or elaborate "get her into bed" scams that do more to divide us than help us connect.

It may not help. But, the way things are going, it sure as hell couldn't hurt.

Chapter Seven

Blessings in the Sky

I have an unfortunate weakness for charming men. I say it's "unfortunate," because I am congenitally unable to distinguish between the good (read: friendly and genuine) Nice Guy kind of charm and the bad (read: smarmy and insincere) Slick-and-Sleazy Mean Guy kind of charm. Oh, hell—I guess it's not that I can't distinguish. It's just that something in my brain chooses not to. All it takes is a husky voice, a blindingly white smile, and a smoothly disarming air and there I am: quivering on the floor in a puddle of gullible goo. Just like the rest of you.

Luckily, I have at least been able to acknowledge this weakness as one of those Five Basic Truths about myself that led to my dating hiatus. I have learned through bitter experience that the kind of slithery charm that comes in handy when trying to bribe a maître d' for a better table in a crowded restaurant is the first step on the highway to heartbreak for your ill-fated dinner companion (i.e., me). So now, whenever I find myself strongly attracted to someone, I always look at him a bit askance before diving in. Because, nine times out of ten, he'll be nothing but trouble.

That, my friends, was the enduring legacy of Larry the Loser: my first official jerk and the man I nearly married.

Larry the Loser was the assistant general manager of a squalid little discotheque around the corner from the real estate office I worked in my first year out of college. Like all of my subsequent jerks, he was *quite* the charmer. He also had three ex-wives, a fierce substance abuse habit, and an aversion to monogamy as deeply ingrained as my attraction to charming men. Of course, I thought he was dashing and promptly moved in with him, much to the horror of my friends and family.

Despite the fact that Larry the Loser was a thoroughly despicable individual, I loved him. He was handsome, funny, and we had a great deal of fun together, at least during the brief periods in which he was able to remain faithful, and we stayed engaged on and off for about five years before I finally realized he was a lost cause, gave up, and moved out.

One of the most endearing things about him was his way with words. Just as he did with the rest of his life, Larry the Loser also made up his own rules about grammar and vocabulary. For whatever reason, he always graced the ends of ordinary words with an extra consonant or two, giving each utterance his own special little flourish. Thus, he never mowed the lawn. He spent his Sunday afternoons tending to our "lawnd." And we never went to his cousin's funeral. We paid our respects to his newly deceased "cousint."

Sometimes he'd just swap out one word for another on a whim, depending on whatever mood he was in. Because he fancied himself a full-blooded Italian (in reality, he only had a tiny bit of Italian ancestry, on his mother's side, three generations removed), he considered himself the only member of our household qualified to stir the Sunday marinara sauce. Only he wouldn't just stir it. He'd "steer" it. Like it was a very expensive luxury automobile that only he could be trusted to drive. And, of course, no family function would have been complete without the enduring spectacle of Larry rushing forward, match aloft, eager to light the flame beneath the towering stainless-steel "coffee urinal."

But my favorite Larry the Loser malapropism wasn't a word at all. It was an entire saying.

Whenever something bad happened to me, he'd always encourage me to try to find the silver lining. Inevitably, he would somehow find a way to wring some good from the situation, and, when he finally succeeded in coaxing a smile out of me, he'd sit back, nod sagely, and say, "Ya see, Lez? I gotta tell ya. What happened, it was a blessin' in the skies."

I didn't have the heart to try to deconstruct the true meaning of the expression "blessing in disguise" for him. I actually liked his version better. It implied a kind of sunny optimism about the world. As if the skies were bursting with good will and happy outcomes, hovering above and just waiting to shower down upon us like so many drops of soft spring rain.

My own "blessing from the skies" actually thundered down in an icy torrent one dreary Saturday morning when a young lady who identified herself as "Larry's girlfriend" materialized on our front doorstep and demanded to be let in. Despite his herculean attempt to convince me she was merely a delusional club groupie who had come by to express concern over his recent head cold, I was unmoved. It's one thing to turn a blind eye to infidelity when you have no direct evidence, but quite another when it's standing in your living room in all its bleached-blond, stirrup-panted, leather trench-coated glory. I moved out shortly thereafter, and thus managed to dodge the bullet of what would have undoubtedly been a brief and miserable marriage.

Now, some guys I know would point to this experience as incontrovertible evidence that all women are only attracted to men who treat them badly, and that any ordinary guy who comes across as too polite and respectful is nothing but a foolish chump destined for a life of eternal bachelorhood.

Sorry, fellas, but it just doesn't work that way.

Believe me, the first thought that pops into my mind when I see an attractive man on the street is not, "Oh! That one looks like he'd steal my car and sleep with my best friend—I choose *him*!"

The appeal of Larry the Loser, and of all jerks, is not that they make us feel bad about ourselves. *Au contraire, mes freres*—they make us feel *good*. They make us feel *special*. They make us feel like there is no one else in the world who is right for them and no other person in the universe who will love them as much as we do. And, in the end, even when they're treating us like complete and utter crap, we still feel special, because, *hey, after all, he's never treated anyone else this badly before! He wouldn't make this much of an effort if he didn't care.*

And so on.

The truth is, women don't like these men because they are jerks. We like them *in spite of the fact* they are jerks. And if you think this is merely a woman thing, by the way, just flip it around and you'll see the same dynamic with men:

If a woman this [choose one] beautiful/smart/funny is paying attention to me, I must really be something on a stick. Yes, I know she only calls me when she wants a free meal or someone to pick her up from the airport, but I'm the one she's calling! She needs me!

> The truth is, women don't like these men because they are jerks. We like them *in spite of the fact* they are jerks.

The conventional wisdom here is that these men fall for such women because they're a challenge. But how is that so different from the perception that women only fall for men who are creeps?

The truth is, there's really not much of a difference at all between men and women when it comes to deciding what we want in a partner. It's pretty simple. We all want what we cannot have and do not want what we can. It's not a man thing. It's not a woman thing. It's a human thing.

Groucho Marx once said he never wanted to belong to a club that would accept him as a member. It's pretty much the same with relationships. Just as it is human to want something we're not sure we can have, it is also human to believe that anything that comes too effortlessly must not be worth having. After all, if

> We all want what we cannot have and do not want what we can. It's not a man thing. It's not a woman thing. It's a human thing.

it's that easy to come by, it must not be very special. Therefore, *we* must not be very special.

The thing about falling in love, though, is that you only need to get it right once. It's a one-in-a-billion shot for some, but sooner or later most of us will stumble across someone who *does* make us feel special, and we'll be pleasantly shocked to discover that the feeling is mutual—which is pretty damn special in and of itself.

As for Larry the Loser, I ran into him from time to time over the next few years, and, although he always vehemently denied it to my face, I learned that he had married Leather Trench-Coat Girl. I have no idea where they are now, but wherever it is, I hope they are happy.

Although you might want to take that last bit with a grand assault.

Married by the Mob

Chapter Eight

Never a Bridesmaid

In all my years of friendships with all the people I am friends with, I have never been asked to be a bridesmaid at anyone's wedding. This may be because my friends are an extraordinarily considerate bunch. Either that, or they simply don't like me as much as I think they do.

The closest I ever came to this . . . uh . . . *honor* was when a friend from high school asked me to do a reading at her ceremony. I was happy to acquiesce, since all this favor required me to do was dress up and appear onstage, two activities I enjoy tremendously regardless of the venue. But, even though everyone else I know has had relatively large weddings, I still have not ever been a bridesmaid.

I suspect this is partially due to the fact that I met many of my current friends long after they had become well established in their lives. By the time they got around to getting married, they'd pretty much filled all the potential slots in their wedding parties. Well, that, and a lot of my friends are male, and I don't care how many Julia Roberts movies you've seen; there is no way any bride is going to relinquish one of those precious berths to someone she secretly believes is a scheming tramp out to steal the groom.

My nonbride friends—and even my former-and-future-bride friends—have all been tasked at least once in their lives with the tiresome chore of tarting themselves up in an ill-fitting fuchsia gown in order to feign enthusiasm over someone's pending nuptials. My poor friend Jessie once had to be in three weddings in a single month, which left her broke, hung over, and perpetually struggling to navigate a closet full of hideous pink shoes. These friends are constantly telling me how lucky I've been to avoid a similar fate, and, while I am inclined to agree, I find it amusing that those most adamant on this point are typically the ones who had the biggest, cheesiest, and ugliest weddings themselves. They are also the ones who were the most apologetic when informing me before their own weddings that I had yet again failed to make the cut. I'd like to think it's because they care enough about my feelings to want to make certain I'm not miffed at being overlooked, but, secretly, I think they simply believe that *their* wedding is going to be the one that's "different." Much the same way they delude themselves into believing that the hepatitis yellow tulle-and-sequined strapless numbers they picked out for their attendants really *can* be worn again.

My friend Sharon was one of these apologists. I had known her through a friend of a friend for approximately ten years but, because I was not a "primary" friend, but

> My poor friend Jessie once had to be in three weddings in a single month, which left her broke, hung over, and perpetually struggling to navigate a closet full of hideous pink shoes.

rather a "friend-once-removed," she "didn't feel right" giving one of the bridesmaid slots to me.

"Maybe I can find something else for you to do," she pondered, tossing out several alarming options ranging from "guest book duty" to "gift collector and labeler" to "helping out with my cousins' children" before I was finally able to convince her I really, *honestly*, didn't mind.

She did, however, invite me to the family reception the night before the wedding, and, because I was having an uncharacteristically good-hair week as a result of a truly spectacular color job that no one has been able to replicate since, I arrived at the event feeling inordinately upbeat and charming. For this reason, Sharon's ninety-year-old Great Aunt Sophie took quite a shine to me, somehow getting it into her head that I was Sharon's maid of honor.

When I gently disabused her of this notion, she frowned mightily, peered at me through her cataracts, and said, "Well, *surely* you're one of the bridesmaids, then."

I smiled as best I could. I like old people, but, honestly, some of them just scare the ever-loving shit out of me. "Nope. Not a bridesmaid. Just a guest."

Great Aunt Sophie reeled backward, gasping, and clapped her hand to her heart. "Oh, but you're so *lovely*! What a *shame*!" Then she turned toward her even-more-ancient sister, who was tottering around among a group of other old ladies about two feet away, and hollered, "Mildred! Mildred!"

Great Aunt Mildred doddered over.

"Look!" sputtered Great Aunt Sophie. "Look at this one! And *she's not a bridesmaid!* Can you imagine? What was Sharon *thinking*?"

Great Aunt Mildred scowled, if not directly at *me*, then at some entity in my general direction. "She asked that horrid roommate—what's her name, the one with the bad skin—instead of *this* one?"

Before I knew it, I was swarmed by a gaggle of clucking, buzzing white heads, all of whom, after inspecting me up and down and surreptitiously scanning the rest of the wedding party for comparative data, pronounced me "a natural bridesmaid," Sharon "a nincompoop," and the marriage "doomed." At one point Great Aunt Mildred even went charging off to find Sharon and right this terrible wrong, but she only made it as far as the dessert table before she had to sit down and catch her breath. Luckily for Sharon, I don't think she stood up again for the rest of the night.

God help me, I was actually rather flattered, despite my puzzlement over the very idea that a less-than-attractive bridesmaid would cause such a stir at an otherwise lovely occasion. Nevertheless, when I repeated the story a few years later, in jest, to another friend who was also apologizing for excluding me from her fourteen-person wedding party, she did not bat an eye.

"Well, I can kind of see that," she said. "You want everything to be perfect. That's why I'm ordering my sister's dress a size smaller than she usually wears. So she'll stick to her diet." When I goggled at her, open mouthed, she bristled slightly and said, "Well, it was *her* idea! She wants my wedding to be perfect, too!"

Now, in fairness to my friend, I do have at least some empathy for what she is going through. Although I've never actually participated in anyone's wedding, I have certainly watched enough of my friends go through the planning process to be well aware of the stress involved. And if I were under that kind of pressure I have a pretty good idea how horrible I would be. *Plenty* horrible, I can tell you that. Hell, I can't even plan a cookout without flying into hysterics over a set of misplaced barbecue tongs; I can't imagine having to plan a five-course sit-down dinner—with flowers *and* a band—for two hundred Great Aunt Sophies. I'd stab my eyes out with a shrimp fork. I know it.

The wedding—that beautiful, perfect wedding—is something we've anticipated since we were old enough to think. And, even though I've never really wanted a big fancy wedding of my own, I still sometimes catch myself thinking, "Well, for *my* wedding I want the rosebud geraniums in peach, not pink. And *no way* will I ever have a deejay—it's a jazz band or nothing." It's *that* ingrained.

I guess this kind of makes sense. Haven't we all been brought up to believe the truest predictor of a successful marriage is the perfection of the wedding? It's the launching point for the Rest of Our Lives; therefore, as long as the wedding is perfect, everything that follows is, by default, going to be perfect as well. That's why

> Relationships, like life, are rarely perfect. But because, somewhere along the line, the mechanics of marriage became the ultimate goal, we never think about what happens once we get beyond the goalpost.

it's all so overblown, from the dress, to the flowers, to the place settings, to the seating charts, to the cake—well, okay, the cake part *is* important. I mean, after all, who doesn't love a good piece of wedding cake?

But, really, does any of that matter over the long run? Relationships, like life, are rarely perfect. But because, somewhere along the line, the mechanics of marriage became the ultimate goal, we never think about what happens once we get beyond the goalpost. There is still a whole life to be lived after the last leftover piece of cake has been boxed up and sent home with the caterer, and it can be an ugly surprise to find out that sharing that life, day in, day out, with a completely different person takes a hell of a lot more work than planning one single day, special as it may be.

That's why, for every two marriages taking place this year, somewhere out there is another couple. A couple who stood up in front of friends, family, Great Aunt Sophie, and eight bridesmaids decked out in sea-foam green chiffon and promised to love, honor, and be faithful 'til death did them part. A couple who, a few years later, realized that perfect day had set such an impossibly high standard that nothing and no one could ever measure up to it. A couple who are unwilling or perhaps unable to confront the perfection myth on which they've staked their entire existence, and either bails on it entirely or muddles along in a state of eternal denial, wrapping themselves in the cloak of superiority and the smug self-assurance that *at least they're married*. No matter how miserable they might really be, at least they've got *that*. For what it's worth, anyway.

The rest of them—the smart ones, the realistic ones, and the truly lucky ones—do suck it up and make it work. Because they've found someone who makes them *want* to make it work. Someone who makes it worth it. The whole of it.

Ugly bridesmaids and all.

Chapter Nine

Warning—Contents May Settle

I have this really convoluted network of friends and acquaintances that has, from time to time, circled back upon itself in all manner of surprising ways. Maybe it's because I've had so many jobs, or because I live in such a small and insular city, but it always seems as though most of the people I know know all the other people I know. If you know what I mean. It's kind of nice, in a way, because it reinforces my perpetual delusion that I am, in fact, the Center of the Universe, and also because it ensures if I go to a party I'll always know at least one other person there.

As far as my friends are concerned, this works out quite nicely for them as well, if for no other reason than our mutual connections all have connections of their own. Which, in turn, leads to an inevitable expansion of everyone's social circles and a plethora of new dating opportunities for one and all.

I once made a friend in an adult education class who subsequently introduced me to several of her friends. One of her friends was a guy by the name of Donald Wheeler, who was, in my opinion, kind of a dork. Nevertheless, because Donald was, like me, the eleventh wheel in his otherwise perfectly balanced social set, my friend thought he and I were meant for each other and went about pestering me to let her fix me up with him.

Now, I try to steer clear of dating friends of friends. No good has ever come of any date arranged or otherwise facilitated by a mutual acquaintance. At best, everyone walks away with bruised egos and a future littered with awkward social interactions. At worst, we all end up hurt, angry, and insulted, lifelong friendships lying in tatters at our feet.

> No good has ever come of any date arranged or otherwise facilitated by a mutual acquaintance. At best, everyone walks away with bruised egos and a future littered with awkward social interactions.

It's not that I don't understand the impulse to try to pair one's friends off as expediently as one can. It's just that the end result is rarely what anyone expects or wants. Better to just leave things alone. Believe me, I'd much rather nurture my friendships into my golden years than suffer through a single evening in the company of some of the individuals my friends thought were my ideal match.

Rather than risk ruining my budding friendship, I deftly pawned Donald off on another friend, Trish. Trish, having just been dumped on her thirty-fifth birthday by her boyfriend of six years, was convinced she was destined to die alone in her cold twin bed and thus leapt at the opportunity to stave off her looming spinsterhood. And, with that, Trish and Donald skipped off, hand in hand, down the rosy road to romance.

They dropped out of sight for a while, presumably to engage in all those romantic coupling activities that seem to be mandatory for every new relationship, and no one was particularly surprised when they reemerged and announced their engagement six months after they met.

After mentally congratulating myself on my stellar matchmaking skills—not to mention breathing a huge sigh of relief that The Donald was now officially off The Market and was thus unlikely to resurface in any of my friends' Bachelors for Leslie pools—I called Trish to offer my best wishes.

"You know," she said, after accepting my congratulations. "You could get engaged, too. I just think your expectations are unrealistic. Meeting Donald made me realize that you really *don't* have to be physically attracted to someone to have a good life. It's much more important to go into marriage with a specific plan. After all, I do want to have kids before I turn forty."

And *that*, my friends, is what is known as Settling.

The world is full of people who have settled, and there's really nothing wrong with the idea in and of itself. I can certainly understand how you would get so lonely, so desperate, and so isolated in a world that seems it was made only for couples that you get to the point where you will make yourself believe just about anything to put an end to your suffering. Many of my friends

> What's wrong with settling is not the fact that you settle. It's the fact that you try to justify settling by insisting you haven't settled at all.

have set arbitrary deadlines for themselves, as in, "I will be married by the time I am forty no matter what!" and, as the deadline approaches, fly into a panic and suddenly decide that the Zima-swilling, bong-toting, tie-dyed Rastafarian they had the fling with seven years ago was really a diamond in the rough and drag me off on a desperate quest through back alleys and dive bars to try to find him and rekindle the flame before it's *Too Late*.

What's wrong with settling is not the fact that you settle. It's the fact that you try to justify settling by insisting you haven't settled at all.

I hear it all the time, from male and female friends alike:

"You know, education is a very subjective thing. I think street smarts are just as important as a high school diploma."

"He only goes to strip clubs because his friends drag him there. I don't have a problem with it. Really. I don't. Not at all."

"She was right under my nose the whole time, but I was just too shallow to see it until the day she got out of rehab."

"He's an athlete—lots of hockey players don't have both front teeth, and why spend the money to replace them when they'll just get knocked out again anyway?"

"My mother was right—I've been way too picky. Loan sharking is a fine profession and I must stop being such a white-collar snob."

We all have our ideals, and they may or may not be reasonable, but there's always something kind of sad about giving up on a dream, however unrealistic that dream may have been. What is even sadder is sacrificing your ideal because of external pressure—whether it's from your parents, your friends, society, or the suddenly overpowering desire to have a warm body—*any* warm body—next to you at social functions.

So, hey, if you're lonely and exasperated and feel like that's the only path you have left, hop on and have at it.

Just don't try to drag everyone else down with you. Don't lecture me about my own expectations being shallow and unrealistic. Don't set yourself up as a shining example of pragmatism and good sense, and then try to insist this was the life you wanted all along. Because, baby, you might as well admit it—you've given up.

And I'm not ready to do that yet.

To me, marriage is a serious business. It's forever. Why shouldn't I be picky? This is the *rest of my life* we're talking about, people! And, at this point, I have garnered enough self-knowledge to be absolutely, rock-solid certain that your little "quirks" that merely annoy me today will drive me to murderous distraction in five, ten, or fifty years. So, believe me, I'm doing myself—and you—a big favor by admitting it now and cutting you loose to go annoy someone who will appreciate it.

Deep down, I really do believe there is someone for everyone out there. Maybe even more than one person. That being said, I don't necessarily believe I'll ever actually find any of them. It takes a daunting combination of courage, perceptiveness, and sheer dumb luck to even stumble across The One, let alone recognize him when you finally do. So, for all I know, I may very well end up a rambling old Cat Lady, living in a basement apartment next to a church and shuffling off at 4:30 P.M. to catch a solitary Early Bird Special at the local Applebees.

But I'm okay with that. And here's why:

For every Trish and Donald, there are ten couples like my friends Cathy and Owen. Ordinary, real-life people with great marriages who *didn't* settle, who *didn't* jump at the first tick of the biological clock, and who love their partners not in spite of their flaws, but because those very flaws are what makes them who they are and are what makes the two of them fit together in that intangible, indescribable way that is so perfect and so right it makes you happy just to be in the same room with them.

And *that*, my friends, is what's worth settling for.

Chapter Ten

Get Her to the Church in Time

From my "This Makes Me Embarrassed to Live in Massachusetts" file:

A woman from a suburb south of Boston made national headlines recently by hosting a public audition on her front lawn to woo prospective husbands for her daughter.

It seems the daughter, a twenty-two-year-old single mother who still lived with her parents, had demonstrated appallingly poor taste in boyfriends (I don't know—but if *my* mother were pimping *me* like a set of secondhand steak knives at a yard sale I might have a bit of a self-esteem problem, too). So the mother, she of the overfrizzed perm and gap-toothed grin, set about to compound the ruin of her daughter's life by throwing open her home to every would-be Aryan skinhead crackpot from Swansea to Salisbury.

Anyone who still believes in that "man shortage" we heard so much about a few years back would do well to read some news accounts of that day's free-for-all. Hordes of delusional young hopefuls lined up around the block for a paper cup of lukewarm lemonade and a five-minute interview with the "selection committee," all the while insisting they were just there out of curiosity.

Or, as one "eligible" young bachelor explained to reporters, "I'm not desperate. Maybe these other guys are, but I'm not."

Note to Delusional Young Bachelor: You have answered a public cattle call in the hopes of winning the hand of a twenty-two-year-old stranger with an overbearing family and questionable taste in men. You are waiting in line to be interviewed by a gaggle of sweat-stained troglodytes sporting mullets and stirrup pants who will, in all likelihood, reject you as "not good enough." And not only are you admitting all this to newspaper reporters, you are letting them print your picture with your real name directly beneath it for all the world to mock. Face it. You're desperate. Also—You're an idiot.

Maybe I've watched too much reality TV, but I was not particularly shocked by this level of tackiness. In any case, I've grown used to people airing their dirty laundry on their front lawns (literally, in this case) for the public at large to pick through and comment upon.

And although I still think the whole thing was sad and pathetic, the cattle call idea isn't what bothers me.

What bothers me is the unquestioned assumption that marriage is this young woman's only path to stability and financial security. Everyone's all up in arms about the means, but no one is paying attention to the end.

This woman is twenty-two years old. She's already saddled with an unplanned toddler she can barely take care of, and now her mother wants to saddle her with a total stranger for a husband when she's barely old enough to legally toast herself at her own wedding.

Let's suppose this scheme does pay off and the Drooling Lawn Herd is winnowed to one lucky contender. Let's suppose he marries her, then abuses her, leaves her, or drops dead. Then what? She'll be right back where she started, or even worse—living at home with her psychotic family, standing in line for food stamps, and trying to raise a daughter who will never have an inkling of what it means to be truly financially independent.

Maybe if she hadn't been brought up to assume that a relationship—*any* relationship, no matter how dysfunctional—

> As long as we continue to teach young women that you can screw up your life innumerable times and it's okay as long as some man comes along in the end to rescue you, they are going to continue screwing up their lives while waiting for that white horse to come galloping up to the welfare office to carry them off.

is her only ticket to stability, she wouldn't have made the horrendously stupid mistakes she already has.

Here's some news: Marriage is not a magic bullet to stave off poverty. Yes, it's difficult to be a single mother, and I know all the statistics about how they are more likely to live in poverty and raise crack addicts than married mothers. But I fail to see how shuttling young women into marriage to the first sucker who happens along is going to make any of these problems go away. As long as we continue to teach young women that you can screw up your life innumerable times and it's okay as long as some man comes along in the end to rescue you, they

are going to continue screwing up their lives while waiting for that white horse to come galloping up to the welfare office to carry them off. And, in the meantime, they'll
put their lives, jobs, and educations on hold while they
run around kissing every frog that hops across their path
in the vain hope he's really Prince Charming in a toad
suit.

Instead of hosting "Who Wants to Marry My
Daughter," maybe they should have gone for something
a bit more practical, like, "Who Wants to Give My
Daughter a College Education and a Job That Pays More
Than Minimum Wage So She Can Become Financially
Independent?"

But it's hard to argue that point when our own government wants to spend 1.5 billion dollars—*billion!*—
pushing marriage on women who are collecting welfare.
It's kind of like the Lawn Auction, but on a grander scale:
It's less about helping a poor, unwed mother make a better life for herself and her child, and more about simply
shunting that responsibility off onto someone—*anyone*—
with a bank account and a pulse.

Now, chop off my ring finger and call me Old Maid,
but wouldn't that $1.5 billion—*billion!* with a *b*!—be better
spent on preventing women from getting into situations
where they feel marriage is their only option? Yes?
Anyone?

I never found out which, if any, delusional young
bachelor actually won the Grand Prize. Maybe it all
worked out in the end and they're all living happily ever
after in a well-kept little cul-de-sac somewhere in the heart
of suburbia. And maybe the toddler in question will grow
up just fine, never absorbing or internalizing the strange

spectacle she witnessed one sunny Saturday afternoon in her grandparents' front yard.

Or maybe she'll draw a different conclusion and end up repeating the sad cycle herself fifteen years from now.

But that's okay, too, I suppose.

After all, who doesn't love a yard sale?

Chapter Eleven

Deconstructing the Married Guy

As someone who has spent her share of time in what passes for the "trendy" bars of downtown Boston, I consider myself something of an authority on the psyche of the men who patronize these venues. This is partially because I've lived in Boston for more than twenty years and feel like I know practically everybody just a little too well, but mostly because, to be honest, Boston has so few trendy bars at any given time that you end up seeing the same people over and over again anyway.

I also travel a lot, and no matter where I go it seems as though I run into the exact same people I encounter in Boston, only with different faces. And, while this sense of overfamiliarity can be more than a little scary—not to mention kind of depressing—I do think it has served me well by helping me stay on my guard in dubious social situations. After all, a bar creep is a bar creep from Boston to Beverly Hills. The only thing that changes is the name of the bar.

> A bar creep is a bar creep from Boston to Beverly Hills. The only thing that changes is the name of the bar.

So, in the interest of sharing the benefit of my cross-country anthropological expertise with the rest of you, I'd like to offer up a little pop quiz to all you ladies out there:

Three guys go into a chic new downtown bar. They're all in their late thirties/early forties. All are reasonably good looking. None is wearing a wedding ring.

Guy #1 is tall, tanned, well dressed, and in great shape. He sits by himself at the end of the bar, and you overhear him say something funny that cracks you up. He notes your amusement, and, because he is friends with the bartender, ends up getting you free drinks all night while regaling you with a host of witty observations about the other patrons, all of whom he seems to know. Before you know it, the two of you have pledged your undying love to each other and you float out of the bar on a cloud of bliss, convinced that, at long last, you have found your perfect soul mate.

Guy #2 is of average height, wearing Levi's, a leather jacket, and a baseball cap. He has a slight beer gut that has not yet progressed from the "cute" to the "just plain repulsive" stage, and he circles you a couple hundred times, drawing a bit closer with each pass, before finally darting in for the kill. During your slightly stilted conversation, he has difficulty maintaining eye contact because he is constantly swiveling to check out the other women entering and leaving the premises, but he does manage to ask you several times if you want to "get out of there" to find somewhere you can "talk." When the tab comes, he offers to split it with you, but, as it turns out, he has forgotten his wallet so you end up paying for the whole thing. And, even though he has taken your business card, you know you'll never hear from him again. And that's . . . *okay*.

Guy #3 is also of average height, but he wears a business suit with an artfully coordinated tie and French cuffs. He approaches you confidently but respectfully, proceeds to ask you all manner of intelligent questions about yourself, and listens attentively to every answer, even cleverly repeating your responses to demonstrate his superior listening skills. He makes you feel like you are the most important person in the world, and when the check arrives he sweeps it up without comment before inviting you out to lunch the following day.

Can you spot the Married Guy in this crowd?

What? Guy #1, you say? Be serious. *He's gay, dummy!* Why do you think you had so much fun together? There was no pressure on either part to turn the encounter into anything more than what it was. No harm, no foul, and you've got a new friend for life.

Who said Guy #2. You? Oh, *come on*. You didn't really pick *him*, did you? You should know better! Pick up that dunce cap and go sit yourself in a corner until you get a clue.

If you answered Guy #3, here's a gold star. Move to the head of the class.

Guy #3 is the Married Guy.

Now, understand this: We're not talking about your average married guy, say, the kind of guy your best friend might be married to—the one who goes out with his buddies for a few beers after work and might even flirt with the bartender if he's feeling particularly daring that night. *That* guy, whether or not you happen to approve of your friend's taste in husbands, is likely a harmless sort.

No. This is *the Married Guy* we're talking about here. The one in the nice tie and French cuffs with the low-key manner and respectful approach who always seems to be hanging around the "in" places whenever you happen to show up.

He's the guy you need to look out for.

The Married Guy is the guy who doesn't wear his wedding ring because he finds jewelry "uncomfortable." Of course, he

> If you want to unmask a Married Guy, check the breast pocket of his suit jacket when he's not looking. You can thank me later.

would never dream of hurting his wife's feelings by letting her know this, but luckily that little gold band is clever enough to wriggle off his finger the moment his car pulls out of the driveway each morning and crafty enough to slip back on as he eases into the garage at the end of the day, so she's never the wiser. If you want to unmask a Married Guy, check the breast pocket of his suit jacket when he's not looking. You can thank me later.

The Married Guy is the guy who can match a shirt to a tie, knows when the double-breasted look is about to go out, and would never dream of wearing running shoes with his business suit no matter how long his daily commute. With a wife at home and maybe a couple of daughters, he's had a never-ending flow of feedback and has thus learned what appeals to women. And don't think he doesn't appreciate it.

The Married Guy is the guy who invites you to lunch instead of, say, dinner and a movie. That's because the Married Guy doesn't want to date you. That would be *cheating*, and, in his mind, anything that might happen between the two of you is just a big accident—an evening between friends that got "out of hand." So he will take you to lunch, because lunch is safe and that is how he will become your friend (unless he invites you to a private lunch in his corporate apartment, in which case he's an old hand who has slithered down the Sleaze Meter from Accidental Philanderer to Utter Scumbag and you should just flee for your life before he sucks you any further into his adulterous vortex). Once the preliminaries are out of the way and you are friends, he will feel perfectly justified in inviting you out for "a drink or two" somewhere (nine times out of ten, the same bar he met you at). From there, it's only a few martinis to the old, "Oh, my God, I was so drunk and you're just so beautiful I couldn't help myself" excuse before he slinks home in the night, never to be seen or heard from again. Until next time, that is.

The Married Guy is the guy who *really* pays attention to you. His interest is not feigned—oh, no, far from it. He really is interested in what you say. First, because it gives him a peek into your psyche to better evaluate your mistress potential; second, because the more you open up to him the more you will come to trust him; and, third, because you represent a refreshing change of pace from the wife-house-kids routine that has been boring him since the day he walked down the aisle. You see, the Married Guy has made a little side-deal with himself in exchange for being the consummate Family Guy on the weekend: During the week, he's a Dynamic Lord of the Universe who hangs around trendy bars with attractive single women who hold more than a passing interest for him. That's his reward to himself for feeling old and stodgy the rest of the time. That's how, he tells himself, he'll keep from turning into his father.

The Married Guy *dabbles* in adultery. Whether he ever actually acts on his impulses is almost irrelevant. To him, it's all a little game. He'll never volunteer that he's married—in fact, he'll do everything possible to avoid mentioning that inconvenient fact—but the moment you confront him he'll freely admit to it. In fact, he'll act like you're the crazy one for ever assuming otherwise. And, once the jig is up, his interest in your conversation will wane as rapidly as it had originally been piqued, and off he'll go, on to the next trendy bar to scope out his next target.

Of course, what the Married Guy fails to take into consideration is everyone else: The wife he fears because she knows his faults and foibles better than anyone. The children he loves yet resents because they remind him on a daily basis of everything he's had to give up for them. And the women he misleads in his singleminded pursuit of self-affirmation who should have better things to do with their lives than star in his tepid little fantasies.

So hear this, Married Guy:

You're starting to piss me off.

You disappoint me.

You lie by omission.

And, most important, you're *wasting my time*.

Married Guy, you are the creep of all bar creeps. You are selfish, immature, and devoid of empathy or kindness. You hurt everyone you touch and you're too self-absorbed to even notice the damage you cause.

Go home, Married Guy. You're not wanted here.

Chapter Twelve

I Don't Know Why
She Does It

I belong to a very nice health club. It's also a very expensive health club, and like all very expensive health clubs, it offers lots of extra perks for its members. There's an onsite bar—very handy for that post-workout cocktail—a swanky restaurant, a health food café, a ridiculously overpriced hair salon (which I have also been known to frequent), a pool, a spa, a movie theater, and an underground garage that offers Premier Members three hours of free parking (which is how I have cost-justified my own Premier Membership, reasoning in a stunning display of mathematical sleight of mind that $25 of free parking per day times five workouts per week actually *makes* me money*).

There's also a daycare center onsite, two floors down from the main club, where all members—regular *and* Premier—can stash their kids for a few hours while they

---

* The ultra-exclusive Premier Locker Room with its personal lockers, big-screen TV, and private concierge did not enter into this equation at all.

take in a power spin or Pilates class. And, up until recently, this arrangement served everyone very nicely: The kids got a place to play, the parents got a nice break, and the rest of us went about our workouts in peace and simply made certain to steer clear of the club during the Sunday Family Hours.

That was why a number of us were so taken aback when the club secretly modified its rules to allow infants and toddlers inside the locker room outside of Family Hours. Supposedly, or so we were told when we discovered this outrage, this was a minor accommodation designed to make things a little easier on all the overstressed moms who needed "more flexible" child-care options.

"Flexible, *my ass*," muttered my friend Jennifer after inadvertently smashing her toe against a giant stroller parked carelessly next to her locker. "The Über-Mommies are behind this. They're taking over the world."

I just nodded in solemn agreement.

The Über-Mommies who frequent our health club are a force to be reckoned with. Smart, organized, and consummately professional in their management of their children's agendas, the Über-Mommies used to have high-powered careers in banking, law, or technology, but they gave them up to stay home with the kids. So now, instead of grooming their professional credentials they have dedicated their lives to grooming their parental credentials by molding the ideal productive citizens of the future. This is a job they attack with the same grim determination with which they tackled college, law school, medical school, and the business world, and woe to anyone who gets in their way.

I sure as hell wasn't going to mess with them.

But what was puzzling me was this notion that the Über-Mommies are so overstressed and frazzled they *need* extra accommodations to make their health club experience less odious. After all, from everything I've been hearing lately, not only are women quitting their jobs in droves to give their all to the little ones at home, they're discovering such untold joy in doing so that we're on the verge of an era of domestic tranquility the likes of which we haven't seen since the turn of last century. Hell, after reading some of the stories in the media about how horrific the life of a working mother is, I was ready to trash my laptop and rush into the kitchen to clean my own oven. And I don't even *have* kids.

> According to the experts, the pressure to be the "perfect" mom is so intense, and the workplace is so inflexible, that no matter what their career status, women across the land have decided it's just "too hard" to have both a job and a family.

According to the experts, the pressure to be the "perfect" mom is so intense, and the workplace is so inflexible, that no matter what their career status, women across the land have decided it's just "too hard" to have both a job and a family. Dr. Daphne de Marneffe, who, in addition to having a last name more apropos to authoring bad romance novels than self-help books, has even written a book arguing that women who work outside the home only do so because they have been conditioned by society (read: feminists) to stifle their innate maternal desires. Far better, she contends, for high-achieving women to stick close to home and hearth rather than try to balance the stress of the working world with the demands of their family.

Caitlin Flanagan, another apostle of the maternalism-over-materialism movement whose own book urges women to "embrace their inner housewife," accuses working women of not only neglecting their children's emotional needs, but their husbands' physical needs as well. And although the loathsome Sylvia Ann Hewlett, author of numerous books and articles touting motherhood as the Holy Grail of human existence, at least offers a token acknowledgment that, yes, some women *have* to work, even she manages to get her digs in at those barren-wombed childless professional woman (i.e., me) while hypocritically clamoring for a more "family-friendly" workplace.

Now, I have no quibble with other people having children, as long as they keep them out from underfoot, muffle their whining, and wipe their noses from time to time. And I have no problem with anyone who wants to quit her job, whether it's to spend more time at Gymboree with the kids or lie around watching *General Hospital* and eating bonbons all day. But I have an enormous beef with those who lobby for a more "family-friendly" working world. Whether we're talking about flex time, "mother's hours," Mommy Tracks, or Hewlett's pet cause, "on and off-ramps" to careers for women of childbearing age, "family friendly" is just a code phrase for "the same old story with a modern-sounding spin."

> Scratch the surface of the "family friendly" rhetoric, and you'll uncover a shockingly retro mind-set that does nothing more than reinforce a status quo that tells us that parenting is, when all is said and done, "women's work."

Scratch the surface of the "family friendly" rhetoric, and you'll uncover a shockingly retro mind-set that does nothing more than reinforce a status quo that tells us that parenting is, when all is said and done, "women's work." Why else do you think they call it "the Mommy Track?" Furthermore, we are told, that's really the way it should be, because motherhood is an innate calling, offering the kind of joy and fulfillment that can only be fully realized by the fairer sex.

But the dirty little secret of this "family friendly" agenda is that it's really *not* designed to make working women's lives easier. It's merely designed to make it easier to continue to foist off the brunt of parental responsibility on women without bothering to acknowledge that there are generally *two* parents in the equation. Sure, we need a "family-friendly" workplace—we need it because women are still stuck with the lion's share of the childcare burden, and there's simply no way we can continue to carry it *and* work full time without one or two token accommodations at the office. Of course, if we had better birth control options, funding for educational programs that build self-esteem in girls so they don't rush out and have a baby with the first guy who says "I love you," courts that actually enforced child support orders, and partners who do more than demand the Congressional Medal of Honor for changing the occasional diaper, we wouldn't need as many of those workplace accommodations. But I guess it's easier to spin all of this as a matter of women's choice.

Unfortunately, the "choice" revolves around the degree of compromise we are willing to endure for the sake of our progeny. After all, women are the ones who are expected to make the personal and professional sacrifices in order to have both a career and a family. We're the ones who have to do the juggling, squeezing in the trips to the supermarket and PTA meetings in between conference calls and sales meetings. And we're the ones who get called selfish for "trying to have it all," or—in my case—all the more selfish for saying, "No thanks, I'll pass."

The Über-Mommies never fail to remind everyone else how selfless and important what they're doing is, usually also throwing in the comment that they "never knew what hard work and sacrifice really was" until they became full-time parents. At the same time, they never stop trying to recruit you into this world of hard work and sacrifice, and no matter how many times you insist you hate children—*all* children, including theirs—they'll just keep mumbling again and again, as if repeating it endlessly will somehow make it true, "It's different when they're yours . . . it's different when they're yours . . ."

> Instead of demanding a more equitable distribution of responsibility across both partners, we look to our employer, our government, or our own inner strength to rearrange the contents of our already straining BabyBjörns.

And why does this happen, you ask?

Because we let it. That's why.

We take the competing interests of work and family onto our own overburdened shoulders, never questioning why it's always up to *us* to do so. We accept the status quo as part and parcel of womanhood, even praising one another for our ability to "multitask" in the face of all this grave responsibility. "If you want something done, ask a woman," is the common refrain—and, instead of demanding a more equitable distribution of responsibility across both partners, we look to our employer, our government, or our own inner strength to rearrange the contents of our already straining BabyBjörns. The end result is, we're twisted up like contortionists trying to adapt, the yokels who knock us up remain the Masters of the Universe, and our bosses suck the lifeblood out of everyone while really only pretending to give a damn.

And, yes, I'm sure there are plenty of nice men out there who really do pull their share around the house. But the whole thing is ass-backward. If we were really serious about achieving a proper work/life balance in our society, it would be universal. We'd make allowances for the fact that we *all* have personal lives that are equally deserving of attention. Then it wouldn't make a difference whether we're taking a personal day to water our plants, feed our cat, or tend to our sick children, because it would be nobody's damned business what we're doing in our off time. *That's* what choice is, my friends. But elevating motherhood over every other life choice does nothing more than reinforce every tired old stereotype we should have done away with by now. And women end up right back where they started: worn out and overstressed, staggering exhaustedly from the kitchen to the cubicle and back again.

Screw that.

If you think I'm going to be the one to have the kids, do the shopping, clean the house, manage the soccer schedule, run all over town to buy Halloween costumes, and punch a time clock to boot, think again. And if you think I'm going to allow myself to get sucked into the Cult of the Über-Mommy, flaunt my superiority over the rest of the world, and devote every drop of managerial might to nurturing what could end up becoming the next generation of Columbine killers, that next generation's going to be a long time coming.

What saddens me more than anything about the choices before me is that, under different circumstances, the Über-Mommies would probably be my friends. In fact, in ten or twelve years they probably will be. By then, they will have long since moved to the suburbs, the kids will be wrapped up in homework, friends, and after-school sports, the husbands will be crawling through trendy bars trying to make lunch dates with attractive single women, and the Über-Mommies will all be sitting around the locker room telling me I don't know how good I have it.

Trust me, ladies. I know.

Chapter Thirteen

I Kid You Not

Memo to Overbreeding Suburban Couple with Screaming Children Who Ruined My Dinner Last Saturday Night: Here are a leash, a muzzle, and a box of condoms. Kindly familiarize yourselves with all of these devices prior to your next public appearance.

I had been looking forward to that evening with my friend Kristin and her husband all week. I hadn't seen them for a while, and the prospect of a nice, leisurely dinner and a nice, leisurely conversation over a nice, leisurely bottle of wine (or two) at our favorite Italian restaurant was far too tempting to forego.

But I could smell trouble the minute we stepped across the threshold. It hung in the air like the rank stench of a day-old diaper.

It wasn't so much that the couple occupying the round table in the middle of the dining room had chosen to bring three very young children (infant included) to a tiny, up-scale, and decidedly NON-family-oriented establishment at 9:00 on a Saturday night. Although if I were a slightly more vindictive soul I might have considered that in and of itself grounds for an anonymous Spite Call to the

Department of Children's Services. Nor did it inconven-ience me too tremendously to have to squish around the ultradeluxe doublewide stroller left carelessly just inside the vestibule. And the world did not come screeching to a halt simply because I came perilously close to slipping and falling on an errant crayon that had somehow man-aged to roll right into my path (thank goodness for sharp-eyed waiters).

No, I really didn't care that they were just outright rude, inconsiderate, horrible people and miserable, unfit, neglectful parents to boot.

I cared very deeply, however, that they saw fit to dis-rupt our dinner, and the dinners of everyone else in the entire tiny, upscale, NON-family-oriented establishment by allowing their most restless (and most vocal) child to prance about, shrieking and capering, from table to table (and, no, while I will occasionally exaggerate certain de-tails for comic effect, in this case the brat really was howl-ing up a storm) while they sat there in oblivious denial, twirling away at their *capellini con zucco* with nary an up-ward glance. And I certainly did not appreciate it when said shrieking child pranced and shrieked her way over to our table, planted herself directly in front of me, and struck a Shirley Temple-esque pose she had obviously been encouraged to think was adorable, but which was, in fact, extremely annoying and not in the least endearing, primarily because she was one of the ugliest children I had ever laid eyes on.

Finally, though, what annoyed me most of all—even more than the shrieking, the prancing, the capering, the posing, and the ugliness—was that when the manager ap-proached the couple and politely asked them to restrain their child, *they refused*. They just outright refused. In fact, they were so offended by the request they unleashed a tirade of wrath and ended up making an even bigger scene than their child had, voices quavering with defensive scorn: "She's just a little girl! Of course she's fidgety! She has to move around! WE'RE PAYING FOR THIS MEAL AND IT'S OUR RIGHT! What's the matter with you? *What have you got against chill-drennnn, anyway?*"

And there it is. The cancer eating away at our society, summed up in one pithy expression of self-righteous outrage:

It's the chill-drennn.

Oh, not the children themselves. Now, while I'll admit to never really having felt even the slightest twinge of that post-forty Baby Fever I keep hearing so much about, I suppose there's nothing inherently wrong with a child. Provided it's kept clean, only brought out on appropriate occasions, and is whisked away at the first hint of restlessness, that is. There are even one or two of them that I actually kind of like.

No, what I don't like about the children is the *parents*.

Today's generation of Alpha Breeders have barged their way into parenthood with the same air of willful entitlement they carry into every other aspect of life. Oh, they say it's about the children, but it's not. It's really about *them*. Because, you see, it's always been all about *them*. And *they* have children, and because *they* have children they have rights! More rights than anyone else!

They have the right to drive the biggest SUV on the planet, because it's safer *for the children!* They have a right to censor television and radio programming for the rest of us because it *protects the children!* They have the right to go anywhere, do anything, and dictate the conduct of everyone else in the country, because, *dammit, they have children!* And the children are our future. The rest of us are just parasites, greedily awaiting the day we'll be able to lie back, put our feet up, and live it up off of the Social Security bounty today's toddlers are destined to provide.

Now, I don't really begrudge the children their due. They didn't ask to be born at all, let alone to the lunkheads who spawned them, so I'm willing to cut them some slack and kick in my share for their upkeep. Besides, the better we tend to the little sociopaths now, the less likely they'll be to murder us all in our beds some dark night in the not-too-distant future. As a result, I support Head Start, universal health care for everyone under eighteen, free school lunches for the poor—heck, if a few extra dollars from my property taxes means a few more after-school programs and a few less juvenile delinquents menacing me on the streets, here's a check. Spend it wisely.

But somewhere along the line, the act of begetting and giving birth to the next generation has taken on an almost religious significance. And, says the always outspoken Sylvia Ann Hewlett in her book *Creating a Life: Professional Women and the Quest for Children*, women like me, who haven't swilled our share of the Kool-Aid, are now ready to come to Jesus. According to Hewlett, who is regularly touted in the media as our nation's foremost expert on "work/life balance," we're all out there banging down the doors of fertility clinics across the nation in a hysterical frenzy because all of a sudden we've realized that we've "waited too long" to have a baby.

Huh?

Hewlett arrived at this staggering conclusion the old-fashioned way: by fudging her statistics. To support the book's main contention, she interviewed 1,400 high-achieving professional women and asked them two questions: First, did they want to have children when they were in college (most said yes); second, did they have children now (most said no). From these answers, she then extrapolated the ludicrous premise that there are millions upon millions of barren-wombed, empty-cribbed professional women out there longing for the unattainable glory that is premenopausal motherhood.

Of course, the question that she pointedly failed to ask was the logical follow-up question that would have likely sent her whole hypothesis crashing to the ground:

Do you regret not having children?

And the answer to that one, my friends, is a little more complicated than a simple yes or no.

Case in point? Me.

When I was in college, I probably did want to have children. Someday. Who didn't? Even though I've never particularly liked children—especially babies, *ick*—I just took it for granted that that was what people did when they grew up. Oh sure, I'd think about whether I wanted boys or girls (boys only), how many I'd have (two), what I'd name them (Geoffrey, and either Benjamin or Sebastian—I never could decide). But I never considered the real question: whether I'd even have them at all. It was just a given, because that's how little girls are brought up. We're brought up to fantasize about the proposal, the wedding, the somewhat-blurry-but-definitely-handsome husband, the beautiful home, the happy family—and, in recent years, the spectacular career on top of it all. We are never given any reason to believe that our lives won't end up that way.

Then we graduated and got lives. We got jobs. We made friends. We took risks. We went on dates—some good, some lousy. Some of us got married. Some of us didn't.

And, yeah, some of us now find that we've pretty much tiptoed through the window of maternal opportunity without really thinking too much about it. And, according to Hewlett, that is a tragedy.

> We're brought up to fantasize about the proposal, the wedding, the somewhat-blurry-but-definitely-handsome husband, the beautiful home, the happy family—and, in recent years, the spectacular career on top of it all. We are never given any reason to believe that our lives won't end up that way.

I'll say it again: *Huh*?

I think it's a far greater tragedy to have a child when you're too young to even know for yourself what the world is really like. Or to have a child with the wrong partner, simply because you're afraid if you don't do it now the clock will run out. Or to have a child that you're not fully prepared to support in the event of death, divorce, or marital disenchantment.

While I have no doubt that many women my age do, in fact, regret that they've never had children, I have to wonder: What is it that they are really mourning? All those unborn children and unfulfilled maternal longings, or that childhood dream of the "perfect" life that they now realize may not quite work for them?

The simple fact is, the little-girl fantasy that we were brought up with is just that—a fantasy. Although many people probably do manage to find a reality that is just as happy or even happier than they imagined it to be when they were in kindergarten, many people don't. And, somewhere along the line, you have to accept the fact that sometimes the dominoes just didn't fall into place the way you expected them to, and then you're faced with a choice: Fly into a panic and do something desperate for the sake of that long-ago fantasy, or say "Oh, well, screw it all" and get on with your life.

And, in getting on with our lives, we make different choices. Different decisions that lead to different experiences. And everything that we have done in order to get on with our lives has made our lives what they are today.

If I had followed Hewlett's prescription, I would probably have been married and pregnant by my late twenties (I'd also most definitely be divorced and waitressing in a truckstop somewhere today; refer to chapter 7 for additional detail). I certainly wouldn't be friends with the people I am friends with, because I guarantee you that I wouldn't have met anyone in my current circle of acquaintances at Larry the Loser's Disco of Debauchery. In fact, if I had had children, *none of the most important events of my life would have ever happened to me*. I would be a completely differ-

> **The little-girl fantasy that we were brought up with is just that—a fantasy.**

ent person—probably someone I wouldn't like very much if I bumped into her on the street today.

So, in answer to the question I asked earlier: Do I regret not having children?

Now that I know what—and who—I'd have had to give up in order to do so?

Hell, no.

However . . .

That doesn't mean other people's choices aren't valid. And, unlike the Overbreeding Suburban Couple who so thoughtlessly disrupted my delicious Italian dinner, I'm not only willing to respect those choices, I'm willing to make some accommodations. I'm ready to build that bridge between the childed and the childfree.

Subject to a few conditions, that is.

Look, I know children misbehave. It's why we *treat* them like children. Every child is a brat at one time or another (and some are brats more often than not). Don't excuse it. Don't tell me it's because they're young, they're tired, they're overstimulated, they're colicky . . . whatever. I don't care what the reason for the brattiness is; as the adult in the picture, it is your job to minimize the impact of said brattiness upon the rest of us. That means accepting responsibility for their behavior, making the appropriate adjustments, and *understanding there are some places you just shouldn't bring them*.

Here's the sad truth: having a child, while a significant event in your life, is hardly the most original thing you can do.

It's what you do with them after you have them that counts.

Chapter Fourteen

The Hardest Job in the World

It has been said that parenting is the "hardest job in the world."

Whoever said that must have been a parent, because I can think of one or two other people who might take issue with that sentiment

Now, don't get me wrong. I've never attempted motherhood, and, at this post-forty juncture, I think I can safely assume I've managed to dodge the maternity bullet for this particular lifetime. And I am quite sure parenting is, at times, challenging, heartbreaking, stressful, and rife with countless moments of unbearable rage and angst. Not to mention the whole going into labor and giving birth thing. Ouch!

But "the hardest job in the world?"

Come on.

> I am quite sure parenting is, at times, challenging, heartbreaking, stressful, and rife with countless moments of unbearable rage and angst. But *"the hardest job in the world?"* Come on.

To me, a "hard" job is one that is physically grueling, psychologically unrewarding, *and* life-threatening. It would involve the ungloved handling of any or all of the following substances: dead bodies, rodents of any sort, giant poisonous reptiles, malodorous body fluids, toxic chemicals, highly contagious deadly viruses, and/or radioactive nuclear waste. Said "hard" job would also offer low or no pay, zero chance for advancement, and a complete and utter dearth of emotional gratification. In short, the "hardest job in the world" would be one that no one, nowhere, under any circumstances would take on voluntarily unless under extreme financial duress or suffering from an acute mental disorder.

Still not convinced?

Fair enough.

As a public service to you all, I have compiled a shortlist of jobs I think could, technically, qualify as "the hardest job in the world." Please note that heading up the neighborhood play group, coaching the soccer team, or even organizing a birthday party for two dozen howling six-year-olds at the local Chuck E. Cheese's, no matter how noisy and stress-infused, all rate a big fat "zero" on the Talbot Occupational Index of Hardest Jobs in the World.

Ready? Let's begin.

✳ *Hardest Job in the World #1* ✳

Guy Who Cleans Out Rendering Vat in Slaughterhouse

Did you know that meatpacking is one of the most dangerous occupations in America? Let's set aside for a moment the inevitable emotional toll on anyone who ekes out a living bludgeoning helpless barnyard animals to death as they whiz by on a conveyer belt and just focus solely on the physical demands of the job, shall we?

Slaughterhouse workers are thirty-five times more likely to die or be injured at work than, say, your typical file clerk. They regularly fall victim to one or more unpleasant conditions, including repetitive stress injuries from performing the same slicing motion up to 1,200 times per day; life-threatening infections from being punctured or lacerated by gore-encrusted cutting implements; gangrene from having limbs crushed and mangled in the rusted gears of faulty grinding machinery; flesh-eating viruses borne by nasty *E. coli* pathogens common to animal feces; and any number of heart, lung, and psychological ailments brought about by the physical, chemical, and mental hazards that rage unchecked through the meatpacking universe.

The worst—and, dare I say, the *hardest*—slaughterhouse job is in the Rendering Room, that foul-smelling inner circle of Dead Cow Hell where they dispose of the extra fat from the animal carcasses. The Guy Who Cleans the Rendering Room must, as part of his duties, actually climb into the vat at the end of his shift to scrape out all the gunk that has accumulated throughout the day. I'll spare you my own grisly musings about what fate may befall the hapless worker who stumbles into the rendering vat before it has drained, but if you're looking for a surefire way to shed those unwanted winter pounds, go buy yourself a copy of *Fast Food Nation*. I guarantee it will frighten you off Big Macs for the next twenty years.

So. Is being a parent harder than being the Guy Who Cleans Out the Rendering Vat in a Slaughterhouse?

Ask yourself this: Would you rather buy your screaming child a Hamburger Happy Meal or die screaming in the rendering vat during the production of said Hamburger Happy Meal?

Don't answer that yet. Let's take a look behind Door #2.

✳ _Hardest Job in the World #2_ ✳

Burmese Diamond Slave

The unfortunate individuals who are sold as slaves into the Burmese Diamond Mines—sometimes by their families, sometimes by corrupt village elders—spend their average workday being starved, beaten with sticks, maimed by machetes, or murdered in all manner of gruesomely creative ways for even the slightest infraction. In addition to physical punishment that includes limb loss by forced amputation, they suffer the emotional battery of either being separated from their families or seeing their loved ones die of the hunger, dehydration, overwork, and internal parasites all too common in Diamond Slavery. After a brief and unremarkable career scrabbling about in a dark, sweltering cave to unearth that perfect token of undying love Skip will drop casually into Muffy's glass of Cristal on that magical night in an upscale restaurant far, far away, our ill-fated Burmese Diamond Slave will likely drop dead from exhaustion at the ripe old age of thirty-two.

So. Is being a parent harder than being a Burmese Diamond Slave?

Ask yourself this: Would you rather slap your child's hand when he misbehaves, or have your hand chopped off when *you* misbehave?

But wait—there's more!

✻ *Hardest Job in the World #3* ✻

Seamstress in Walt Disney Sweatshop

Yup. You read that right. The Walt Disney Company, those kindly old souls who bring us Mickey, Minnie, Goofy, and the rest of that jolly band of cartoon capitalists, is also one of the most egregious exploiters of subcontracted (read: sweatshop) labor in the world.

Visit any Disney store, or go to their Web site, and you will see a dazzling selection of Disney collectibles—hats, T-shirts, sleepwear, toys, dolls, stuffed animals, snow globes, whatever—across which frolic the smiling visages of your favorite Disney characters. In order to keep this bounty of overpriced paraphernalia flowing into its retail outlets, Disney subcontracts the labor on a piecework basis to an assortment of poorly managed, multiethnic sweatshops dotting the globe from Haiti to Indonesia.

What do you know—it *is* a small world after all.

The next time you head out to buy little Timmy a new pair of Cowabunga Mickey Swim Shorts, take a moment to offer up a silent thank-you to the fifteen-year-old girl who hand-stitched them. Chances are, by the time she got around to your item she had already worked a twelve-hour shift inside a hot, stuffy warehouse that gives new meaning to the word "firetrap," locked in alongside hundreds of other women and children who take turns using one of the two overflowing toilets on their too-infrequent bathroom breaks. After she finishes little Timmy's Cowabunga Mickey Swim Shorts, she'll work for another six hours and then, after a dinner consisting of rice, maybe some beans, and a couple of soggy vegetables, she will collapse into a triple-decker bunk in yet another locked warehouse, wedged in among her tubercular, lice-infested co-workers. All for the U.S. equivalent of three dollars per week, from which is deducted the cost of her meals, such as they are; lodging, such as it is; and any accumulated fines for such heinous transgressions as missing quota, being late, or trying to escape.

Oh, and by the way, my publisher would like me to point out that the Walt Disney Company does not own, operate, or endorse these types of facilities and hence has no knowledge of or legal liability for the manner in which these facilities are maintained. There. Consider yourself disclaimed.

So. Is being a parent harder than being a Seamstress in a Walt Disney Sweatshop?

Ask yourself this: Would you rather struggle to get your little boy into his Buzz Lightyear PJ Pals, or struggle to get out from under a smothering, flaming pile of Buzz Lightyear PJ Pals?

I thought so.

We are all prone to hyperbole from time to time. Lord knows, there are certainly days when I feel as though an empty inbox or a looming deadline makes my job the hardest one in the world. But you will never catch me running around telling other people that for the sole purpose of making them feel bad about their own jobs. Or to make myself feel better about a choice I have freely made.

So the next time you have a rough day in the car-pool lane, do me a favor. Stroll over to your jewelry box, slip on your DeBeers three-stone diamond pendant, bundle the kids into the Land Rover, and take them for a quick spin through the nearest drive-thru. And when you get home, tuck them into their Tinkerbell Pixie Power flannel sheets, give them a good-night kiss, and sit back for a moment to bask in the glow of their fresh-scrubbed, rosy-cheeked, unconditional love.

Then go downstairs, pour yourself a nice glass of Merlot, and try to convince me again just how hard your job really is.

Chapter Fifteen

Proprietary Values

From my "This Makes Me Proud to Live in Massachusetts" File:

On November 18, 2003, our Supreme Judicial Court ruled that same-sex couples have a constitutional right to legally wed.

This was kind of a good news/bad news event for just about everybody, inside and outside our little Commonwealth. Good news for my gay friends, who can look forward to two bridal showers and double the wedding gifts; bad news for Yours Truly, who will have to attend said showers and pay for said gifts. Good news for the Red State politicians, who are galvanizing their constituents around the specter of marriage licenses being issued to depraved individuals seeking to marry their brothers, sisters, pets, houseplants, or all of the above; bad news for the Massachusetts politicians, who are scrambling around trying to figure out how they can take a position on the issue without offending any of their constituents. Bad news for the homophobes and religious freaks who are worming their way out of the woodwork faster than a nest of termites during a house fire; good news for the Catholic Church, which gets to pretend to be relevant again and is thrilled to have found a big new rug under which to sweep its own egregious violations of privacy and sexual boundaries.

To me, the idea is pretty much a no-brainer. Either you favor equal rights for gay people or you don't, and if you don't then you're acknowledging you think they're somehow less than full-fledged citizens. Granted, I'm not particularly religious (okay, I'm not religious at all), but, to me, most of the concerns I've heard expressed about same-sex marriage are religious in nature, and, as such, ignorable.

They're also totally specious, and since they have already been shredded to bits by all who are wise and rational, let's just dispose of the following right off the bat: that God created marriage for procreative purposes only (infertile and/or childless couples need not apply); same-sex marriage is an un-Christian environment and thus unfit for raising children (I'm sure Andrea Yates's kids would love to come up for air to add their two cents); and that same-sex marriage is wrong because homosexuals are aberrations of God (I'm not sure whether there is a God, but if there is I'm quite sure He's a little more on the ball than that and would certainly have noticed and fixed His mistake at some point in the last FIVE THOUSAND YEARS).

What surprises me, though, is how many of my own friends are troubled by the issue. And they're not particularly religious either—off the top of my head I can only think of one or two who actually even go to church every week.

They're not worried about the decline of morality, the eventual dissolution of the human species, the hordes of morally corrupt toddlers gearing up to march upon our nursery schools, or entire suburban neighborhoods bursting into flames under the fiery wrath of the Almighty. No one I know buys any of that. But, for some reason, the idea of same-sex marriage makes a lot of them feel all squicky inside, and even the most liberal among my non-gay friends have a hard time articulating why.

"I don't know . . . It just makes me uncomfortable."

"It doesn't seem . . . normal. Why can't they just live together?"

"I don't think we should change the definition of marriage. It's too important. It's too special."

And there it is. The real reason behind the ambivalence, the angst, and the all-around agonizing over the same-sex marriage issue:

Spite. Plain old childish, immature, petty spite. They simply cannot abide the idea that something they have built up in their own minds as the be-all, end-all of human existence can be done by Just Anyone. Someone who doesn't *have* to do it in the first place.

Many—not all, but a fair amount—of the people I know who got married did so simply because they decided it was Time. They had reached a certain age, wanted to have children, or had arrived at a critical juncture in a relationship where friends, family, obligation, and convenience dictated it was time to settle down and hitch up with whomever was waking up on the next pillow. And boom—six weeks later they were filling out bridal registries under the approving gaze of Mom, Dad, and Mr. Williams-Sonoma.

Maybe, just maybe, what's really going on here is a simple case of envy. Maybe these folks are so protective of their proprietary rights over the institution of marriage because they see in same-sex couples a freedom of choice they have never, will never, know. And maybe they begrudge them that freedom.

The same-sex couples I know are together not because they're *expected* to be, but because they *want* to be. They don't have to contend with the same kind of pressure we straight people do. It's not like Aunt Ethel is hovering over her lesbian niece urging her to "find a nice gal and settle down in Northampton, already!"

I think this drives some people absolutely batty.

Look, everyone wants to feel special. Everyone wants to be important. Everyone wants to think that they have something, or are a part of something, that sets them apart from the huddled masses. There's always someone who wants to lord it over someone else, and if you ever even insinuate that what he's doing is somehow less special, less distinguishing, less exclusive than he would like it to be, he'll fly into a frenzy and will howl and rant and rage against any interlopers who even try to infringe on his turf. And we have all been brought up to believe that there is *nothing* more special, more important, than finding someone—*anyone*—to settle down and raise a family with. It's the Most Important Decision we'll ever make; ergo, it is a privilege that shouldn't be awarded to Just Anyone.

> The same-sex couples I know are together not because they're *expected* to be. It's not like Aunt Ethel is hovering over her lesbian niece urging her to "find a nice gal and settle down in Northampton, already!"

But isn't that the point, really?

To me, marriage *is* a Big Frigging Deal. Why do you think I'm not married? It's far too important to entrust to Just Anyone. So when I see two people who actually manage to have a good relationship, I *want to* root for them. I *want* it to work out. I don't care if they're gay or straight—I just want to believe that, somewhere in this world, love and commitment actually exist on a level that surpasses the boundaries of societal expectation.

But if you really want to start placing qualifications on that degree of commitment, I suggest that before you start picking on the homosexuals, you start at the bottom: with the wife beaters, the adulterers, the child abusers, the serial monogamists, and then move on to everyone else who derives

> Do any of you seriously believe that we, in all our supposed heterosexual superiority, truly value the so-called "specialness" of marriage? Have you *seen* what's on TV these days?

an unwarranted sense of superiority for participating in an institution that, for all the rhetoric to the contrary, they really don't value all that much anyway.

Do any of you seriously believe that we, in all our supposed heterosexual superiority, truly value the so-called "specialness" of marriage? Have you *seen* what's on TV these days? Can you sit there and tell me that you've managed to channel-surf through *Married by America, Trading Spouses, The Bachelor, Who Wants to Marry My Dad*? Have you checked the divorce statistics recently? Didn't we just try to plunk 1.5 billion—*with a b!*—dollars into promoting marriage to the unwilling? Do you honestly believe homosexuals can do a better job screwing up the institution of marriage than we have already?

Do you?

Because when it comes to screwing up the institution of marriage, believe me—two guys picking out china patterns are the least of our problems.

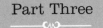

Part Three

A Culture of Strife

Chapter Sixteen

Mars and Venus Go to Hell

An urgent bulletin from the Department of the Apocalypse: Satan has gotten himself a diploma-mill PhD and is now walking among us in the earthly form of Dr. John Gray.

Who?

For those of you who have been living in a cave for the last decade, Dr. John Gray is the evil mastermind behind the inexplicably popular "Mars and Venus" franchise. You know, how "men are from Mars, women are from Venus," and all our problems with the opposite sex are simply a result of opposing natures and conflicting communication styles.

Still confused? Well, allow me to explain:

According to Dr. Gray, men are fierce Martian Warriors. They are direct, problem-solving, action-oriented commitmentphobes who long to roam free across the land, hunting, pillaging, and scattering their seed in a testosterone-fueled frenzy.

Women, on the other hand, are gentle Venutian goddesses—sensitive, loving nurturers who talk endlessly about problems without ever actually solving them, longing instead for the perfect soul mate who will help fulfill our true desire to remain indoors, sheltered and secure, tending to home and hearth.

It's all very pretty and poetic, and, as pop psychology goes, hangs together quite nicely in our faith-based culture of dumbed-down metaphors. And the fact that there is not one shred of empirical proof to support any of his theories has not kept Dr. Gray from turning this sizzling heap of crap into a multimillion-dollar industry. In addition to all the books—I think there were eleven or twelve of them at last count—there are also cassettes, videotapes, a Web site, a syndicated advice column, a radio show, a board game, a *musical* (!), and an entire curriculum of workshops, seminars, certification programs, and couples-coaching sessions, all brought to you courtesy of Lucifer's Death Star, i.e., the Mars Venus Institute at www.marsvenus.com. There was even a TV talk show for a while, hosted by that treacherous gender-sellout Cybill Shepherd, whom I actually used to like before she bowed down to the Beast and had the Mark of Venus branded on her sensitive, nurturing forehead.

True confession time: Back when I was in my early thirties and still convinced I needed to renounce my shallowly singular ways, I actually purchased—in hardcover, no less—a copy of *Mars and Venus on a Date*. I'm almost too ashamed to admit this now, but I bought the book on the basis of a single chapter heading that caught my eye: "Why Some Women Are Still Single."

The logical fallacy that underlies the entire premise was not readily apparent to me at the time. I mean, think about it. There are roughly the same number of men and women on the planet, aren't there? So it stands to reason that, if there are so many single women out there, there are bound to be one or two *men* in the same situation, no?

Where's *their* chapter?

They don't have a chapter! They don't have a chapter, you see, because the book wasn't really written for them. And if you go to Dr. John Gray's Web site (don't go; please—you've just got to trust me on this one, okay?) you'll see that, for all the psychobabbly blather about the mutuality of this communication breakdown, the lip service paid to "working it out together," and the pseudo-sociological emphasis on "openness and honesty," none of this so-called advice is really meant to be followed—or even consumed by—men. Despite the fact that it has been exhaustively documented by numerous (real) experts that there are just as many, if not more, unhappily single men placing ads and joining dating services as there are women, every single book, Web site, TV show, magazine article, advice column, and how-to video is directed at women and women only. That's why they all have pink covers, play sappy background music, or offer "beauty tips" along with straight-from-the-can relationship advice.

And we buy it. We buy it all. We buy it all because we have been conditioned from birth to believe we are solely responsible for managing and sustaining our relationships. Men, according to the Tao of Gray, are what they are and they're not capable of anything better. It is up to us, we are told, to understand them, accommodate them, humor them, and adapt our own expectations and behavior accordingly. All the better to trick them into settling down with us.

In *Mars and Venus on a Date*, Dr. Gray opines that the real reason "some women" (i.e., me) are still single is that we are unwilling or unable to convince the men we go out with that we actually "need them." We frighten them. We are too independent. We don't have to be "rescued." They don't know how to cope when we're not twittering after them to change our oil, take out our trash, and slay the woolly mammoth so we can skin it, cook it, and serve it up for a candlelit dinner.

Or, as Dr. Gray so earnestly puts it, "What good is a knight in shining armor when you're slaying your own dragons?"

Once you've wiped the giant chunks of projectile vomit off your shoes, riddle me this: As insulting as this whole premise is to women, isn't it even more insulting to men? I mean, at least Dr. Gray is giving us credit for being able to change, but apparently, the way he sees it, men are a lost cause.

And he's not the only one. According to every self-styled relationship pundit, be it Dr. Gray, the Rules Girls, Robin Norwood, or any of the rest of that merry old band of quacks and hacks, men are so foolish and malleable that all it takes is one or two clever mind-tricks and a quick stroke to that fragile ego and boom—they're down on one knee, ring in hand, ready to pop the question.

Apparently this is a tremendously difficult lesson for us high-achieving ball-breakers to learn. Luckily, there's no shortage of helpful hints out there for that desperate woman approaching forty to use to get a man to rescue her from certain spinsterhood. To spare you all the chore and expense of actually acquiring any of these materials yourself—not to mention the shame of having to explain to your IT department why "www.catchhimand-keephim.com" popped up on your company's Web server with your IP address attached—I have compiled a handy list of dependency tips from a variety of media, both traditional and electronic. Feel free to refer to them whenever you need to make your man feel powerful and in control. You can thank me after your honeymoon.

Dependency Tip #1: Ask him to help you take your cat to the vet. Because EVERY single woman owns a cat, right? Okay, well, I do own a cat. But that's beside the point. Still, it's always a good idea to demand that the poor schmuck you've been dating for the past couple of weeks wrestle little Fluffy into the kitty carrier in preparation for that lengthy trek to the neighborhood veterinary center. The first vet visit is an important step in the coupling process that has the added benefit of making him feel like he's the strong and powerful patriarch of your little pseudo-family. I'm sure he will think of you—and Fluffy—quite fondly as he lies sprawled in the gutter, lifeblood gushing out in a crimson flood from the hundreds of claw lacerations inflicted upon him by your terrified pet. Perhaps, since you can't rescue a gal any more effectively than by dying for her, he'll even have time to propose before he bleeds to death. At least then you can say you were engaged once.

Dependency Tip #2: Ask him to take you car shopping. Now *that's* a brilliant idea! Of course, it presents an even trickier conundrum for the most high-status of ballbreakers—those executive-level overachievers who might want to splurge on that nice new Mercedes with the convertible top, OnStar, and twelve-disc CD changer. Sending your future husband storming out of the dealership in an intimidated snit is probably not the most effective way to bolster his tenuous self-esteem. Best stick with a safe, inexpensive "chick" car—a Volkswagon Beetle, a MINI Cooper or, if you want him to think you have a touch of the rebel in you, a Mazda Miata. Better yet, pretend you're ready to fritter away your pin money on something completely mechanically impractical! Just pull down a list of bad car choices from the Internet and "casually" run them by him for his opinion. He will welcome the opportunity to chuckle indulgently at your charming naïveté before setting you up in that nice, safe, Honda Civic his buddy's wife is itching to unload. And if his automotive savvy leaves something to be desired and you end up in a clunker, so much the better! Now he'll have even more chances to rescue you. Every time you break down.

Dependency Tip #3: Ask him for advice about a troubling work situation. Your work environment offers a limitless bounty of dependency scenarios—but be selective when choosing which one to focus on. Don't ever consult him about compensation issues; the last thing you want to do is let on you make more money than he does. Similarly, you should never sound him out on anything concerning your staff. A needy woman doesn't have a staff—she IS the staff! And, above all, never, ever, ever, under any circumstance, present him with a *real* problem you are wrestling with, such as whether to up the production quota for the Topeka facility if the gross domestic product increases by more than .5 percent next quarter. There's a good chance he may not be able to solve it, and then he'll just resent you for making him feel bad about himself. Nope. When consulting with your man on matters of employment, simplicity is the name of the game: Just tell him your boss yelled at you. If you can squeeze out a tear or two while choking out your sad story, you'll be that much ahead of the game. Not only will he have the opportunity to comfort and advise you, he'll undoubtedly concoct any number of brilliant revenge fantasies that although never actually acted upon will nonetheless keep him entertained for weeks. Either way, he'll wind up appreciating you all the more.

> If I follow these rules, it's likely I'll end up with nothing more than a selfish, egocentric, spoiled-rotten little man-child who is so gullible he actually bought my act and so insecure and needy that nothing I do will ever make him happy.

Of course, there's always the chance that, if I were to try it, the needy approach might actually work. And what then? What will I have achieved in the end? In exchange for sublimating my personality and selling my very soul in the hopes of finagling my way into a wedding gown, *what am I really getting out of the deal?*

If I follow these rules, it's likely I'll end up with nothing more than a selfish, egocentric, spoiled-rotten little man-child who is so gullible he actually bought my act and so insecure and needy that nothing I do will ever make him happy. Oh, I'll do everything the pundits tell me I should do—let him think he's the Master of the Universe, quit my job if he wants me to stay home with the kids, keep my figure through yoga and Pilates, and even have my face done when I hit fifty.

Then I'll spend another twenty years sitting home alone while he's out getting his frail Martian ego stroked by yet another ex-high-achieving ballbreaker ten years my junior who is following the Seduction Guidelines for Aspiring Trophy Wives in Dr. John Gray's latest bestseller: *Mars and Venus Have a Back-Alley Affair*.

But, hey, there's always a bright side. At least I'll be married.

Chapter Seventeen

Grating Expectations

What is it with you researchers in Michigan, anyway?

Is it a conspiracy? A well-orchestrated campaign to upset me? The work product of a year-end convention in Kalamazoo during which you all sit around and brainstorm ever more creative ways to get my dander up?

Or are you all really just this stupid?

Not content to merely saddle me and my shallowly singular ways with sole responsibility for the destruction of the environment, sociologists in the Wolverine State have launched a new salvo in their ongoing crusade to terrorize single women across the nation. According to the latest study, this one by Stephanie Brown of the University of Michigan, we successful single women might as well chuck those college diplomas and high-paying jobs right out the office window, because as long as we've got them, men won't want us. When selecting a mate to settle down with, she says, odds are the fellas will be hooking up with the secretary, not the boss.

According to the flurry of press reports that accompanied the release of these "fascinating and timely" findings, this study provides definitive proof that powerful women are SOL* when they hit the marriage market.

It's merely evolution in action, says Ms. Brown: Men prefer less accomplished women, she explains, because they fear the more powerful ladies will be unfaithful, thus jeopardizing their mates' chances of passing those jealous little chromosomes on to the next generation: "This pattern is consistent with the possibility that there were reproductive advantages for males who preferred to form long-term relationships with relatively subordinate partners."

Apparently, it's safer to go for the less ambitious gals, because the more dependent the woman is on the man's earning power, the more likely she will be to stay in the kitchen and be sure to have supper on the table at 6:00 P.M. sharp. So men are "biologically programmed" to gravitate toward women in subordinate positions in the workplace: the receptionists, the flight attendants, the cocktail waitresses, and the like. All the better to maintain mastery over their teeny, tiny . . . uh . . . *domains*.

My question: *Who are these guys, and why would any self-respecting professional woman want to marry one of them in the first place?*

Any man who is that afraid of being cuckolded before he has a chance to spawn will be snowblowing me a parking space in Hell before his insecure spermatozoa get anywhere near *this* overachieving womb. But, based upon the media flurry around Ms. Brown's findings, I guess I should just shut up and take what I can get, because if I

---

* Shit out of luck.

make more than $19K this year I'll be lucky to snag a tattooed ex-con with two teeth and chronic halitosis, let alone the CEO of a Fortune 500 company.

Ordinarily, I would dismiss this study out of hand as yet another one of those hysterical predictions of familial Armageddon that sweeps through the national zeitgeist every couple of years. Much like that long-discredited terrorism study from the eighties that had young women trampling one another in a rush to the altar for fear their chances of marriage would plummet below zero if they waited until after their thirtieth birthday to tie the knot. Unfortunately, the Michigan study came on the heels of still more dubious "scholarship" out of the United Kingdom that purported to show how the incidence of marriage decreases by 40 percent for women for every sixteen-point increase in their IQ, whereas the reverse is true for men. In other words, we are warned in a tone of dire foreboding, men don't want to marry smart women any more than they want to marry successful ones.

I guess nobody stopped to wonder whether maybe the marriage rates are dropping because *smart women just don't want to marry stupid guys*.

In any case, what puzzles me about this whole brouhaha is, even if it were all true, what, exactly, are women expected to do with this information? Drop out of high school? Quit our jobs? Feign a learning disability? *What?*

Since we can't very well lower our IQs, I suspect we are being urged to lower something else instead: our expectations. After all, the more selective women become, the less likely we will be to settle for an unfulfilling relationship. And if we are less likely to settle for an unfulfilling relationship, one of two things will happen: either we don't get married at all, or men will fly into a panic and start working a little harder to become worthy of *our* attention. In either case, the little pink engine of guilt, fear, and insecurity that powers so much of the female contribution to our economy would require a drastic retooling. And that, blusters everyone from George W. Bush to Jerry Falwell to the loathsome Sylvia Ann Hewlett, would be . . . get ready for it . . . *Anti-Family!*

And now, suddenly, everything makes sense.

Now I know why TV shows are overrun with beautiful, intelligent women trapped in sexless marriages to dumb, schlumpy men who behave like even bigger children than the passel of precocious brats they've somehow managed to sire. *Get used to it, ladies,* the networks hiss. *Jim Belushi is your last best hope, so suck it up and make him a snack, bitch!*

Now I know the secret of the self-help industry: Follow the Rules and subscribe to the Tao of Mars and Venus, because any man who is still pursuing you even after all the coy little mind games those books require you to put him through is either an obsessed psycho-stalker or a sad little doormat with bad skin and an overdeveloped Oedipus complex—in other words, an ideal match for today's desperate I-Wanna-Be-a-Housewife.

And now I know why, everywhere I turn, the message is the same: Do not expect men to meet your level of goodness. Do not expect them to treat you well. Do not expect them to be faithful, or intelligent, or to behave like adults.

They don't know any better, so it's up to you to compromise, to teach them right from wrong, to tell them how to dress and buy their clothes for them, and to carry the entire weight of the relationship yourself. They are not responsible. So just grab onto the first one who happens your way and start with the procreating, because based on the new conventional wisdom, you're not likely to get a second chance. Hell, you were lucky to even get this one.

Oh, and you'd better make sure you look good while you're at it. Here. Buy another fashion magazine and try the Grapefruit Diet before you pack the kids into the minivan for another trip to Chuck E. Cheese's. *Ch-ching!*

The pressure to compromise, to give in, is so unrelenting we don't even have the time to sit down and ask ourselves whether it's even worth it. Is having a mate—any mate—really worth the superhuman sacrifice it takes to secure one?

> Is having a mate—any mate—really worth the superhuman sacrifice it takes to secure one?

I decided to go straight to the source for my answer. If Stephanie Brown's research subjects were, in fact, the new gurus of female acceptability, I reasoned, I should at least try to find out a bit more about them. Who is this "typical man," I wondered, who is so timid, so frightened, so locked into his rigid little gender role he runs squealing in terror from the very notion of feminine accomplishment? And if his opinion carries so much credence in the world, perhaps he is a better catch than I originally thought. Maybe I was missing something!

So I looked up the information about the study online. Here's how it worked: The researchers showed participants photographs of various men and women, and then asked then to rate each subject's desirability based on his or her hypothetical work relationship with the participant (peer, boss, assistant, etc.).

Oh, and the entire research sample consisted of undergraduate students in the 18–22 year age range, whose sum total experience with the opposite sex was likely limited to body shots at the frat house keg party.

These are the men we are weeping over?

The frustrating thing about all these studies is they only deal in hypotheticals. Put a series of what-if scenarios in front of a person, and, yeah, he might very well respond in a way that is predictable. That's why they're called stereotypes—they had to originate somewhere. But I suspect that reality is far more nuanced. Ultimately, you fall in love with someone because of who that person is, not his or her relative position on the company org. chart. The odds of this happening increase proportionate to the amount of life experience you bring to the party. And then those characteristics that seemed so essential when you were twenty—*my future wife must be petite, blond, Catholic and worship the ground I walk on*—completely evaporate when you connect with someone on a level you heretofore never even imagined existed.

Or you can just stick to that original plan and spend the rest of your life screening out those hypothetical "undesirables," never stopping to ask yourself what it is, exactly, that makes *you* such a catch.

So forgive me if I don't rush off to Receiving and Discharge at the Massachusetts State Correctional Institution to snap up the first new parolee who slouches into my sights before some other single forty-something sinks her grasping claws into the scruff of his scruffy neck. She can have him, and I'm sure she'll consider her-self lucky to get him.

After all, the less she expects, the less likely she is to be disappointed.

But that's only because she expected so little in the first place.

Chapter Eighteen

He's Just a Big Fat Asshole

As if the all-too-prevalent image of that lonely single woman waiting anxiously by the phone for the call that never comes isn't pathetic enough, now there's a new phenomenon sweeping our Singular Nation:

According to the newest breed of relationship experts, mixed signals, refusal to commit, disappearing and reappearing acts—classic signs of what used to be called commitmentphobia—are not, in fact, indications that men are (choose one):

- Conflicted

- Scared of being hurt

- Intimidated by our fabulousness

Nope. There's really a much simpler explanation for all the ambivalence and inconsistency in men's behavior: *They just don't like us very much!* And apparently we need a whole slew of pundits, talk shows, and magazine quizzes—complete with both multiple choice *and* essay questions—to tell us so.

When I first heard about this newfangled spin on the oldfangled topic of Men Behaving Badly, it seemed like a splendid idea to me. I'm all for giving people the unvarnished truth, and, wimp that I am, would be more than happy to have a best-selling author or two do my dirty work for me. But I know myself. And I know lots of women just like me. And something about this whole idea just rankled me, and I couldn't put my finger on the reason for my skepticism until I did a little digging on Amazon.com. And then it hit me:

Hidden beneath that innocuous-sounding "he's just not that into you" message lies the subtext that every smart, professional, well-educated single woman is really just a delusional would-be stalker. Is this true? Is today's average woman so addled by love and blinded by desperation she hallucinates relationships that never existed, reads amorous subtext into every innocuous comment, and fixates so relentlessly on some ephemeral fantasy of romantic bliss that she's poised over the stove, match in hand, ready to light the flame beneath a giant kettle of Family Pet Stew at the merest flicker of polite attention?

> Hidden beneath that innocuous-sounding "he's just not that into you" message lies the subtext that every smart, professional, well-educated single woman is really just a delusional would-be stalker.

Nah. I'd say it's far more likely that she believes a relationship is there because she's been *led to believe* a relationship is there. She hears that amorous subtext because there *is* an amorous subtext. And she's caught up in that romantic fantasy because *someone has been feeding* that romantic fantasy. And who could that someone be?

Hmmm. I wonder who. Could it be . . . *the Big Fat Asshole who led her on in the first place?*

Where's *his* book?

Now, over the course of my dating life I've done my share of rationalizing and making up excuses as to why some men have treated me badly. But the operative phrase in that sentence is "treated me badly." In other words, the delusions and rationalizations I may harbor about any given man who may have disappointed me are usually in direct response to some sort of misleading behavior on his part. But, according to the conventional new wisdom, it's not really his fault at all: Even the most notorious players are actually deep-down swell guys who are just as lovelorn as the rest of us. They simply have yet to find their Soul Mate. And, what with "men being men" and all, anything they say or do in search of said Soul Mate, no matter how thoughtless or inconsiderate, is not only to be excused, but should actually be *expected*. The only inkling we ever get that there might be something wrong with the man in the equation is generally a parenthetical reminder buried toward the end of whatever book or article happens to be dealing with the topic that, yes, some guys are, in fact, absolute slugs who are beyond redemption and best left to their own devices.

Oh, and by the way? *They're* just not that into us, either!

I think even the original proponents of the "he's just not that into you" hypothesis would agree that bullies, rageaholics, and freaky sexual deviants are indeed Big Fat Assholes. But what no one else seems to grasp is that a lot of these other so-called nice-but-conflicted guys are really Big Fat Assholes, too.

So how can you tell the difference? In case you're still having trouble figuring out if he's worth it or not, allow me to further clarify for you:

The guy who insists on giving you his phone number but never bothers to return your calls? Big Fat Asshole.

The guy who only calls you when he's drunk and disappears the moment the sun comes up? *Really* Big Fat Asshole.

The guy who's been living with you for five years and constantly weasels out of setting a wedding date because he's "just too busy at work?" Say it with me, people—*Big Fat Asshole!*

The guy who promises to call after a really great first date but never does? Big Fa—oh. Wait a minute. Actually, he's probably *not* a Big Fat Asshole. More likely, he was just telling a polite little white lie so as to not hurt your feelings and end the date on an awkward note. That was actually kind of nice.

But as for the rest of them . . .

There is something very wrong in a world where women must be constantly warned to not trust men. Where we are scoffed at, patronized, and condescended to because we have committed the unpardonable sin of actually believing the men we fall in love with are honorable and noble. Where we have to buy books—*dozens of them!*—to disabuse ourselves of the expectation that someone who may only be interested in us on a physical level might actually be a decent enough person to understand that it's not nice to exploit our feelings by pretending to feel something that's not there just to get us into bed, and who therefore will refrain from doing so.

Instead of constantly having to play defense, wouldn't

it be nice if, just once, we could actually hold people accountable for the promises they make—explicit or implied—rather than shrug our shoulders saying, "Well, that's just the way men are. We can't expect any more from them, and if we fall for their line it serves us right because we should have known better."

> Instead of constantly having to play defense, wouldn't it be nice if, just once, we could actually hold people accountable for the promises they make—explicit or implied—rather than shrug our shoulders saying, "Well, that's just the way men are."

True, we rationalize bad behavior on the part of those we love all the time. It's a defense mechanism for getting over heartbreak, and we do it because *it makes us feel better*. Why obsess that someone broke up with you because he thought your nose was too big and you laugh like Nestor, the Long-Eared Donkey when, instead, you can just tell yourself he was so overcome by your charm and wit he felt too unworthy to be in your presence for one second longer? Left to your own devices, you'll get over it and move on to someone who appreciates you, hee-haws and all.

But the key to recovery is being left alone. And any guy with any shred of integrity whatsoever will respect that. Because, believe me, they may be confused or ambivalent about a lot of things, but there are two things they do know: They know they don't reciprocate our feelings, and they know that to pretend otherwise is just a cruel and terrible lie.

So if he's still stringing you along with a lot of vague promises or relying on you for a surefire ego boost when he's feeling down, I recommend you give him *my* book.

No, not this one.

The one entitled *Don't Be a Big Fat Asshole: The No-Excuses Guide to Behaving Like a Decent Human Being*.

With my compliments.

Chapter Nineteen

A Manly Pursuit

Okay, okay. I know what you're thinking. I can practically hear it: *Oh, Leslie, you're so myopic!* For every unfair stereotype and unrealistic expectation on the part of men I point out, I'm sure there are at least a dozen of you out there in the penis gallery itching to remind me, "You know, it's not just men! Women can be Big Fat Assholes, *too-oo!*"

For the record: Yes, I know. I'm probably one of them. In fact, I'll even cop to that time in college I pretended to like this guy because he said he would fix my car in exchange for a dinner date. I took him to the International House of Pancakes and then left him at the closest subway stop. (If it makes you feel any better, it turned out he had completely fried my transmission, my dad had to drive all the way up to Boston to take charge of the repairs, and I received a sound scolding on the importance of regular automotive maintenance beginning with, "It's a good idea to check your fluids more than once every three years.")

But, look, I'm a woman. Most of my friends are women. Of course my opinions are going to skew female. And, since women are routinely expected to carry the weight of our relationships, odds are we'll have better stories to tell anyway.

Nevertheless, I am a reasonable person. I have no problem injecting a little fairness and balance into my ordinarily biased brand of punditry. So I agree: It's high time I take a little stroll over to the other side of the locker room and put my fingers to the keyboard in defense of the rougher sex.

Fellas, this one's for you.

A good deal of time and energy have been expended in recent years in an effort to discern just what the heck it is women want from men anyway. People of both sexes are confused, we are told, because the feminist movement has so thoroughly emasculated the male of the species the poor things now believe a Phillips-head screwdriver is a new kind of vodka martini served in gay bars.

It's our fault, they say, because we give men mixed signals. We claim to want sensitive, understanding "nice" guys who hold the door for us and pick up the check, but in reality we have a secret hankering for motorcycle-riding, leather-jacketed "bad boys" who not only won't pick up the check, they'll leave us stuck with it after they sneak out the back door with the cocktail waitress. Men have turned inward in response, choosing to indulge themselves with shopping sprees, facials, and pedicures rather than subject themselves to the shallow whims of the fickle female. They've become, not quite gay, exactly, but a curious hybrid of the homo and hetero persuasions. They have become . . . metrosexual.

Or so we thought, until the good people at Harris Interactive exploded the myth by asking 1,003 men and 1,128 women what *they* believe are the most desirable characteristics in a man. Turns out, if the screeching headlines are to be believed, the metrosexual is dead. "Manly men" are back.

This, of course, begs the question: Are the 1,003 men who find manly men desirable manly men themselves?

The brain, it sizzles.

This question didn't seem to faze the media, who, as usual, simply spun the story as a failure of feminism: "Hold the Quiche! Manly Men Are Back in Vogue!" shrilled the *Washington Times*. "Goodbye, New Man, Welcome Back, Mr. Rough and Ready!" the *Weekly Telegraph* proclaimed in glee. The Independent Women's Forum went even farther, sniffing "Despite MTV and the New York City culture being hyped in mainstream media, it's not how most American women view life and the opposite sex."

> If acting like a sulky bastard is all it takes to be deemed a metrosexual, I'd be hard-pressed to recall an occasion when I *wasn't* dating one.

One thing's for sure: Given that the Harris respondents have assured us that "dependability and a sense of humor" are now the two most important qualities in the manly man, we *can* safely assume that those surly, unreliable guys who were all the rage last year are now yesterday's news.

Gosh, if acting like a sulky bastard is all it takes to be deemed a metrosexual, I'd be hard-pressed to recall an occasion when I *wasn't* dating one.

Now, I'm glad the metrosexual is out, primarily because, honestly, it's damned hard to date someone more vain than you are. You're so busy jostling for a space at the mirror you end up never going anywhere. But am I really the "manly man" kind of gal? And, more importantly, since this is your chapter, guys, should I be advising all of you out there to go ahead and embrace your inner simpleton so as to increase your appeal to the opposite sex?

There's only one way to find out: Let's examine the evidence.

Personal Appearance: According to the Harris poll, Manly Men buy their grooming products at grocery stores and drugstores, whereas metrosexuals buy their grooming products at hair salons. Score one for the Manly Man. Sharing a hair salon with your significant other is just bad karma all around. Larry the Loser, my infamous ex, and I went to the same hairdresser because she gave us a "couples" discount. She also knew he was cheating on me three months before I found out because Larry actually referred his new girlfriend to our hairdresser in the hopes of getting an extra third off. And he got it! I was so furious when I found out I fired the hairdresser on the spot, and it took me a good five years to find someone else who foiled as well as she did. You can bet I'll never make a mistake like that again. It's too risky. When weighing the comparative anguish inflicted by a bad relationship versus bad hair, I'll gladly suffer the former to avoid the latter. Score: Manly Man: 1. Metro Man: 0.

Hobbies: Still more good news for the Manly Man: He not only spends his spare time on home improvement projects, he actually enjoys doing them! So, apparently, in addition to the irresistible lure of a freshly painted bathroom, it's easier to get a date with Manly Man—all I need to do is to walk up and down the street brandishing a plunger and asking random attractive guys if they know how to use it. Although I must say, just because I don't want to unplug my own toilet doesn't necessarily mean I want to date the guy who does. A metrosexual actually cares about where his hands have been—and, frankly, so do I. Yep. Given a choice between a guy wielding a blow-dryer or the guy snaking my sewer pipe, I'm going to go for Mr. Conair every time. Score: Tied.

Entertainment: This one should be easy. The Manly Man eschews designer clothing and prefers to spend his spare cash on home electronics. Now *there's* a guy after my own heart. What better test of a couple's commitment to one another than an entire weekend spent wiring up a brand-new home theater system? Sorry, metrosexuals, but trolling the aisles of Bloomingdale's for the latest in Joseph Abboud just doesn't compare to the joy of a perfectly tuned HDTV. But, wait—what's this? The Manly Man would rather watch *sports*? What about all my boxed-set TV show DVDs? I still have three seasons of *NYPD Blue* to get through! Score: Forget it. On to the tiebreaker.

Tiebreaker: According to the survey, 90 percent of the female respondents claim to want "low-maintenance, easygoing men." I assume that's code for "manly." Hmmm. Are the other 10 percent of us running around out there saying, "Goddammit! Where have all the whiny, demanding, hard-to-please men *gone,* anyway?" And what, exactly, do "low-maintenance" and "easygoing" actually mean? Aren't those awfully subjective terms? Who really decides these things? *Who is the arbiter of true manliness?*

Turns out, it's Dodge Motors.

Dodge Motors commissioned the Harris poll.

You know Dodge. The company that aggressively markets its environmentally challenged megatrucks to the "man's men" among us and once even ran a joint promotion with Home Depot promising, "Power tools for him; a nice kitchen and bathroom for her."

I swear to God, I couldn't make this stuff up if I wanted to.

Nevertheless, there you have it, guys. Your path to manliness—if you choose to take it.

Oh—just one more thing before you decide.

By some shocking coincidence, the manliness poll results were "announced" just as Dodge was getting ready to announce the winner of their "Dodge Dakota Ultimate Guy" competition. The "Dodge Dakota Ultimate Guy" is someone whose "bold, distinctive, style" and "unique capabilities" make him "stand out from the crowd." The winner will be deemed "truck-worthy" enough to win a new Dodge Dakota and tickets to "local sporting events" for him and his "buds."

Hmmm. What does "truck-worthy" mean anyway?

Oh! Wait—I know! MANLY. Right?

Amazing, how it all comes together, huh?

Chapter Twenty

Read It and Weep

Back when I was a starving college student, I hit upon a brilliant moneymaking scheme: I was going to write romance novels under an assumed name.

It wouldn't be that difficult, I thought. I'd always gotten good grades in English. I enjoyed writing. And, from what I had seen, all one had to do to write a successful romance novel was follow a very simple formula:

Beautiful heroine (not conventionally beautiful, but with unusual looks that make her stand out; also, she's spunky) meets handsome (fill in one): **PRINCE, KNIGHT, CONQUEROR.** Complications ensue due to interference from evil (fill in one): **WARLORD, KING, SORCERESS** who wants (fill in one): **HEROINE, HERO** for (fill in one): **HIMSELF, HERSELF.** Couple reunited after (fill in one): **NOBLE SACRIFICE BY HERO, CHANGE OF HEART BY VILLAIN, SWORD FIGHT.**

It was like Mad Libs, except dumber.

The romance-novel strategy ended up being a little too ambitious for a full-time college student to take on, and, after researching the arduous process of becoming an author a bit further, I decided it would be more practical to just write other students' term papers for money.

Technically, I was supposed to be tutoring people, but I've never been a very patient teacher and eventually found it more expedient to just write the damned things myself so that I could get the session over with and go out drinking.

After I graduated and had been in the working world for several years, I decided it was time to get serious about writing again. This time, I vowed, I would write a *real* novel, not some cheesy piece of romantic drivel. So I put together the beginnings of a very witty (I thought) story about a charmingly clumsy marketing director with a disastrous love life who was determined to get engaged within a year. It was fluffy and breezy, and I shared it with a few friends, who pronounced it "hilarious" and begged me to write more. I didn't. I set the manuscript aside when I realized I didn't particularly like my heroine and thus had no desire to inflict her annoying habits on any of my male characters in order to provide the requisite happy ending.

A few months after I jettisoned the novel, my friend Jennifer called me with some stunning news. "I just bought this *hysterical* book!" she announced. "You have to read it—it's just like yours!"

I was, admittedly, curious. And a little jealous that someone had beaten me to the bookshelves with an idea I still considered my own, however unjustifiably. So off I went to the bookstore to check out the competition.

And that was how I discovered *Bridget Jones's Diary*.

Now, here is my shameful secret: I bought that book. I enjoyed that book. I laughed along—quite heartily, I might add—with that book. And, when it became clear what a huge best-seller that book was going to be, I even considered dusting off my own manuscript and riding Helen Fielding's coattails to fame, but decided not to bother—after all, I scoffed, who would ever want to publish what would, by that point, be considered nothing better than a second-rate copycat job?

Shows you how much I knew about the publishing industry back then.

Less than three months after Bridget hit the States, the bookshelves were overflowing with *Bridget Clones's Diaries*. Irresponsible shopaholics and resentful nannies vied for our attention with nascent fashion editors and would-be business moguls, and the cash registers *ch-chinged* their ringing testament to the collective appetite for this type of fiction. It even became its own genre: Chick Lit.

Since I had enjoyed Bridget's exploits in spite of myself, I bought several Chick Lit books. Some of them, I actually read. Eventually, however, I found myself growing as annoyed with the Chick Lit heroines as I had with my own. I found the characters insipid and their travails little more than exploits in stupidity.

More than anything else, though, I just grew bored with the same old plotlines:

Beautiful heroine (who doesn't consider herself beautiful but, based on the cover art, usually is; also, she's spunky) with (fill in one): **FABULOUS CAREER, SLAVELIKE ENTRY-LEVEL JOB** in (fill in one): **BUSINESS, PUBLISHING, FASHION** meets handsome (fill in one): **BOSS, CO-WORKER, NEIGHBOR**. Complications ensue due to interference from evil (fill in one): **BOSS, EX-GIRLFRIEND OF HERO, PRETTIER BUT UNSTABLE SISTER, JEALOUS ROOMMATE** who wants (fill in one): **HERO, HEROINE, HEROINE'S JOB** for (fill in one): **HIMSELF, HERSELF**. Couple reunited after (fill in one): **HEROINE QUITS FABULOUS CAREER TO MENTOR CRIPPLED CHILDREN, HEROINE IS PROMOTED OUT OF ENTRY-LEVEL SLAVELIKE JOB.**

Oh, and there are always shoes. Good Lord, we can't forget the shoes.

Chick Lit novels are the Harlequin Romances of our times—with one important difference. With a romance novel, you know you're reading fiction. Bad fiction, granted, but fiction nonetheless. The settings, plots, characters are so unrealistic that, if you are inclined toward that type of entertainment, you will be amused, entertained, and then promptly forget the book the moment you put it down. It's pure escapism, unconnected to our daily life.

> But, by creating settings, plots, and characters much more in line with our everyday experiences—but not *quite* as banal—Chick Lit not only Harlequinizes our lives, it also not-so-subtly reminds us that our own lives aren't quite up to snuff.

But, by creating settings, plots, and characters much more in line with our everyday experiences—but not *quite* as banal—Chick Lit not only Harlequinizes our lives, it also not-so-subtly reminds us that our own lives aren't quite up to snuff. Forget the shoes, the designer outfits, the "fabulous" settings. These are staples of every fluff novel and can be appreciated and/or laughed off with little fanfare. But Chick Lit, in all its incarnations, gets at us where we live. The one place we thought we were safe. Our oasis from the relentless grindery of the relationship industry.

Work.

Suddenly, it's not enough to have a decent, well-paying job we enjoy and are good at. We must have a *glamorous* job—or a job on the fringes of a glamorous profession—that throws us into close personal contact with millionaires, heiresses, and people with their own airplanes. And we *absolutely cannot* be a star performer at our workplace: We must screw up. A lot. And charmingly. Preferably, in front of the millionaires, heiresses, and people with their own airplanes.

Most important, we cannot just have good working relationships with our colleagues—there must be at least one in whom we have a romantic interest. Because, in Chick Lit, romance is everywhere. That is the only way a job can be exciting, so we must be constantly on the lookout now for that stray encounter at the vending machine that will lead to this millennium's version of happily-ever-after. Work used to be the last refuge of the single person against the relentless pressure to couple up—now, even that boundary has been crossed. We've gone from fiction-as-escapism to work-as-fiction.

And, in the requisite happy ending that is a staple of the Chick Lit novel, professional success is not an end in and of itself. It is merely another path to romance. Whatever life lessons the protagonist learns, whatever confidence she gains, whatever career advancement results from whatever happens to her, if it's not accompanied by a fulfilling relationship it is all for naught. Success for its own sake is not sufficient. That's why you see so few true Chick Lit heroines with "serious" careers—the consequences of giving up a "serious" career for the sake of romance are far too profound to be glossed over in a mere fifty thousand words.

And that's the real downside of Chick Lit: By ranking all our accomplishments on the basis of the romantic success that arises from them, it minimizes the importance of those accomplishments. Nothing else we do matters— there's no happy ending worth celebrating—unless there's an engagement ring at the end of the rainbow.

I still have my old manuscript, sitting in a folder at the bottom of a plastic file box beneath my bed. About two years ago, I actually took it out and reread it and was surprised to discover it wasn't half bad. I wondered whether I could do anything to it to make it more meaningful, so I sat down at my computer and attempted to update it.

After about ten pages I sat back and reviewed my draft and realized that what I had written bore very little resemblance to the breezy, fluffy story I had begun all those years before. Turns out, I was exceedingly annoyed at the state of the relationship industry and, rather than write a lighthearted piece of fiction, I had instead generated a lengthy opinion piece detailing the multiple offenses the relationship industry was committing against single people.

Hmmm. Interesting. One of these days, I ought to do something with that.

Chapter Twenty-one

Remote Acceptability

Here's an interesting factoid about myself that's sure to impress even the most hardened gender warriors: The male of our species may indeed be the Master of the Universe, but *I* am the Mistress of the Universal Remote.

That's right. Using *only my right thumb*, I can operate every piece of home entertainment equipment in my entire apartment with a single remote control. For those of you who are interested in such things, this includes the following: two television sets; two digital cable boxes with Comcast OnDemand programming; two TiVos; one DVD recorder/player, two VCR/DVD combo players; one Bose 3-2-1 radio/CD/DVD system, which controls the audio for all the components in my living room; and one Bose Wave Radio/CD Player, which controls the audio for all the components in my bedroom.

This weekend I'm going to sic it on my light switches, too.

Touch me. Go ahead. Feel my power.

This superior mastery (mistressy?) of all things electronic was acquired with the assistance of a marvelous little device called the Harmony 880 Universal Remote, available for an extortionary fee at your friendly neighborhood Best Buy.

You've seen the universal remotes they sell in other places: enormous, boxy contraptions with row upon row of tiny, hard-to-read buttons too small for anyone with a finger larger than a two-year-old's to press. They come with instruction manuals the size of the Verizon Yellow Pages, which boast two-sided sheets of badly translated English on one side and badly translated upside-down Spanish on the other. I have never known anyone to be able to successfully program one of these behemoths to do more than turn their TV set on and off, let alone take advantage of all the fancy functionality so tantalizingly described on the package.

The Harmony 880 Universal Remote is different. It comes with a USB cable that plugs into your computer, and you can program it using software you download from the Harmony Web site. All you need are the brand names and model numbers of all your various components, a detailed understanding of how they all work together, and a whole lot of patience.

Since I have a necessarily overcomplicated but nonetheless functional setup sporting a variety of multicolored cables that pass my digital signal through five separate devices before it reaches my TV, I was quite convinced the Harmony 880 Universal Remote would never live up to its hype. Sure, it might be able to figure out that I need to turn on my Bose 3-2-1 system to hear the audio from my Daewoo flat-screen TV—really, what self-respecting universal remote couldn't get that far? But how would it ever know that, to get a picture from the Daewoo flat-screen TV, my Phillips DVD recorder/player must be on, but my Sony DVD/VCR combo unit must be off? How could I explain that I watch DVDs from the Phillips DVD recorder/player on Channel 4, but DVDs from the Sony DVD/VCR combo unit on Channel 3? And how in the name of Our Sweet Baby Jesus would it ever master the intricacies of the TiVo Keyword/Title Search?

Well, after a few days, almost an entire case of Diet Coke, and several thousand tweaks, I finally managed to get the Harmony 880 Universal Remote to do all this and more, and, when finished, happily dispatched all the other remotes to an old box in a lonely corner of my under-TV cabinet, where they will accumulate dust until such time as I run out of AA batteries and need to raid the Device Graveyard for functional spares. Then I settled back into the soft cushions of my oversized green TV chair, popped open the last can of Diet Coke, and watched TV until my eyes turned red. In the course of a single day, I devoured two DVDs I had received from Netflix three months earlier but had yet to open until that moment; my favorite episode of *Law & Order: Special Victims Unit*, which I had stored on an old VHS cassette and tucked into the back of my bookcase; the *Daily Show* I had TiVo'd the night before; and the three final episodes of *Six Feet Under*, courtesy of HBO OnDemand.

I even tried to trick the Harmony 880 Universal Remote a few times by switching from device to device in rapid succession to see how smart it was, and became irrationally proud of it when it saw through all my clever little traps and adjusted itself accordingly.

I had just finished calling my family and all my friends to boast of my brilliance and to tell them to not bother inviting me anywhere ever again because I had no reason to leave my apartment for the rest of my life, when I decided to give my Harmony 880 Universal Remote a well-deserved break and picked up the newspaper. And therein I learned that, not only had I gone about my purchase decision in completely the wrong way, I had committed an egregious act of gender treachery to boot.

The article that short-circuited my little electronic bubble was a perky little tome in the Living/Arts section explaining to all and sundry the concept of WAF. That's home electronics lingo for "Wife Acceptance Factor," the latest electronics purchasing trend sweeping the nation. According to the article, I didn't actually spend sixteen hours programming and reprogramming my Harmony 880 Universal Remote because I enjoyed the challenge of mastering a fascinating piece of technology that would ultimately help my home entertainment system operate more efficiently, not to mention give me bragging rights among my fellow videophiles for years to come. Nope. Apparently, I only bought the Harmony 880 Universal Remote because it's . . . *pretty*.

Women, as per the "experts" at Best Buy and Circuit City, as well as two squabbling couples the reporter accosted on the sales floor of the local Wal-Mart, want home electronics that look nice. We buy tiny stereo systems in silvery tones because they blend in better with our home decor. Whether or how well they work is but an afterthought. Men, however, are the true arbiters of power and functionality. They long for black, bulky, wide-screen HDTVs that remind them of Battlestar Galactica, and couldn't care less how many wires they have to trip over to get to the on switch. If it's big, noisy, and has a lot of cool features, they're all for it. And, according to these same experts, this dichotomy has spawned a new concept in the never-ending battle of the sexes: the Wife Acceptance Factor.

In the World of WAF, men are commitmentphobic technophiles who chafe at domesticity and crave the power only a giant subwoofer can provide, and women are the shrill harpies hellbent on civilizing them. Up until they marry, we learn, men are carefree sprites who enjoy toys, golf, and weekend tailgate parties. But then, alas, forced to set aside their childish pursuits for the good of the family, they are swallowed up in the looming shadow of WAF. One man in the article carried on as though his wife had ripped a small puppy from his arms and drowned it in their bathtub in front of the children, simply because she objected when he secretly spent their joint savings on a 42-inch plasma TV that only he wanted. To hear him tell it, she made him return the big TV because it was ugly. The concepts of selfishness, stupidity, and outright thievery apparently never occurred to him.

Will anyone ever put a stop to this constant drumbeat from the media that women are genetically predisposed to tame the male beast, and men are overgrown children who must be mothered into grudging submission? Women are the nesters, or so the conventional wisdom goes—the iron-willed matriarchs who dole out sexual favors in direct proportion to how well their husbands toe the domestic line. And, like all good mothers, we control the toys.

The problem with this scenario, of course, is that it completely denigrates the male contribution to the adult relationship. Instead, it absolves him of all accountability for his own actions and places the responsibility for his behavior squarely on the shoulders of the woman in his life.

As if we didn't have enough to deal with already.

I have to admit, I felt pretty silly after reading the article and thinking about all that time I wasted scouring CNET for product reviews and customer comments. I should have spent those hours on a more gender-appropriate activity, like picking out a flat-screen TV I could hang on my wall with a lovely floral-print frame around it.

At least it's good to know in advance what I am in for should I ever decide to marry. My future husband will be an aesthetically clueless boor with a hankering for two gigantic speakers and the call of the open road. I'll have to nag that right out of him.

I'd write more, but, to be honest with you, I'm a bit distracted by my computer. It's very large and ugly, you see, and it's surrounded by all these messy wires that mar the stark symmetry of my perfectly dusted desktop. I am far too uncomfortable with this visual assault on my delicate sensibilities, so I think I'll just toddle off and play with the multicolored buttons on my new Harmony 880 Universal Remote.

Pretty . . . shiny . . . oooooo . . .

Chapter Twenty-two

Profiles in Scurrilage

You might not know it to look at me, but I am a very dangerous character.

Behind the briefcase, underneath the power suit, and just below the surface, I am a walking, breathing menace to our nation's security.

You see, I am a single female.

The national security implications of my marital status came into question last week, when, while embarking on a day trip from Boston to New York, I was selected—yet again—for one of those so-called "random" personal screenings at the gate to the Delta Shuttle.

Now, I'm all for heightened vigilance at U.S. airports. Frankly, I'm just happy *someone's* paying attention, and I have little patience for the whiners (read: white businessmen) who complain that transportation security policy is "too PC" and that we should, instead, focus on catching the "real" terrorists (read: nonwhite leisure travelers). But it did strike me as rather odd that, ever since September 11, the number of times I have been selected for that so-called "random" personal screening has easily exceeded the number of times I have been waved through the metal detector unchallenged. And, after a while, it does get a little embarrassing to see your underwear emptied out onto the counter in full view of your fellow passengers while you are being publicly "wanded" by burly female Transportation Security Administration screeners. Plus, given how long it takes my laptop to boot up for the requisite "it's not a bomb" inspection, and how imprecisely I tend to calculate the length of time it takes me to get to the airport, I run a significant risk of missing my plane every time I am pulled out of line.

My friend Kathy, also a frequent business traveler, gets selected even more frequently than I do. We were discussing the phenomenon over cocktails one evening, and the guy sitting next to us, who claimed to work for one of the airlines, overheard the conversation and chimed in, "You must each travel alone a lot."

> "Single women who travel alone are searched almost as frequently as Middle Eastern men who travel in groups."

"What do you mean?" I asked.

"Single women who travel alone are searched almost as frequently as Middle Eastern men who travel in groups," he told us.

"Why?" Kathy demanded. "Is that how the male security guards get their thrills?"

"Hell, no," said the guy. "It's all done by computer. They ran some algorithm a few years back that flagged single women as high-risk travelers because they're more likely to be duped into carrying drugs or explosives for their boyfriends." He looked pointedly at Kathy and added, "Blondes especially."

Kathy and I looked at each other in horror.

We've been profiled!

Granted, I have no idea if what he told us is true. But it would certainly not shock me if it were. After all, the Lonely and Gullible Single Woman is so prevalent in today's culture, it's not surprising our government believes we'd resort to terrorism in exchange for dinner and a movie on Saturday night. We're desperate enough to fall for anything!

Troll through your television listings any time of day, any day of the week, for a sense of how pervasive this depiction actually is. On the twenty-four-hour news channels, running ticker tapes scroll out the fates of deluded white women who have disappeared at the hands of the charming sociopaths they were foolish enough to love, while over on the networks dead victims of serial killers in prime-time crime procedurals vie for airtime with bubble-headed reality show contestants who prattle cluelessly about romantic "connections" and "love at first sight."

But nowhere is the desperation of the gullible more stunningly—and ruthlessly—depicted than in the Made for Television Movie for Women.

The Television Movie for Women has dealt a withering one-two punch to the single woman's equilibrium, first by reminding us how miserable our lives are without a man, and then warning us how much worse off we'll probably be if we do ever manage to find ourselves one. That's because, nine times out of ten, the villain in the picture is the Too-Good-to-Be-True New Boyfriend, who sweeps us off our feet with declarations of love within forty-eight hours of meeting us and only reveals his true intent—to ensnare us as reluctant pawns in his nefarious schemes—

after we are too besotted to turn him down. Even if we do manage to get a marriage proposal out of him, it's only to further his plot along, and there's usually an extra wife or two stashed out of state to nullify the marriage before the end credits roll. So not only were we stupid enough to marry a criminal, we weren't even really married to him to begin with!

In any case if I'm to believe the made for TV movies (and apparently, the U.S. government), the choices that lie before me as a single female are bleak indeed: Either I'm doomed to spend my life sitting around on my sofa in sweatpants eating cookie-dough ice cream straight from the carton, or I risk falling victim to any or all of the following sad fates:

Stalking: My Too-Good-To-Be-True New Boyfriend, so loving and attentive at the beginning of our relationship, will suddenly become a full-fledged citizen of the Republic of Crazy and launch a rapidly escalating pattern of stalking behavior that includes tapping my phone, hacking into my computer, and sitting in a parked van outside my apartment staring up at my bedroom window through night-vision goggles. Oh, and if I have a pet—forget it, it's a goner. While being stalked, I will do tremendously stupid things, like break into his apartment and discover conveniently scrapbooked news clippings reporting his recent escape from the maximum-security psychiatric facility he was confined to after being convicted of a series of stalking-murders in his hometown. I will do these tremendously stupid things because I "refuse to live like a victim." Of course, I *will* be a victim in the end—or damned close to one—unless the detective in charge of my case is moved by my plight, takes a romantic interest in me, and shows up in time to save me from my own foolishness.

Prostitution: I will be sweet-talked into joining a high-end "escort service" by my Slick New Boyfriend, who just so happens to own said high-end "escort service." At first, everything will seem very glamorous and exciting, and I won't really mind the "whore" part too much because all the customers really want to do is take me out for a nice meal and some good conversation. Eventually, however, someone will want me to sing for my supper to a drastically different tune, and when I balk, my Slick New Boyfriend will either wheedle me into continuing or, if he is also a Slick and Bullyish New Boyfriend, just smack me around until I do what he tells me to. My career as a high-class hooker will come to an abrupt end when some fatherly businessman (who might actually *be* my father if the movie is exceptionally daring) who has inexplicably tried to avail himself of my services, makes me feel bad about myself. After a violent confrontation with my Slick and Suddenly Cowardly New Boyfriend, I'll quit. Miraculously, none of this will trouble my Long-Suffering Boring Ex-Boyfriend, who will be moved by my plight, declare his continued romantic interest in me, and pledge to help me pick up the pieces when I go crawling back to him.

Smuggling. I will be duped into smuggling drugs by my Mysterious New Boyfriend, who will have secretly sewn ten kilos of cocaine into the lining of my suitcase hoping I won't notice the extra weight (I won't). I will also most decidedly *not* be selected for a so-called "random" personal screening before boarding the plane—which will be my bad luck because I *will* be apprehended by customs authorities the moment I disembark and thrown into a brutal foreign prison. Justice will finally prevail when the vacationing American lawyer who just so happened to witness my arrest is moved by my plight, takes a romantic interest in me, and secures my release.

Swindling: I will be swindled out of my life savings by my Flamboyant New Boyfriend, whose Ferrari and designer suits were financed courtesy of a string of other Lonely and Gullible Single Women who also fell victim to his stock scam. If he is really evil, the Flamboyant New Boyfriend will trick me into getting my friends and family into the act, and I will only learn the truth when one of his other marks shows up at my front door to warn me off. The police will refuse to investigate, save one dogged SEC investigator who will be moved by my plight, take a romantic interest in me, and help me turn the tables on the schemer. I will manage to get my friends' and family's life savings back, but my own money will be gone for good. Lesson learned.

Blackmail: I will be blackmailed by my Sleazy New Boyfriend, who has secretly planted video cameras in my bedroom and shower. He will use the tapes to force me into embezzling money from my company, or, if I work at a bank, engineering a robbery. I will have no choice but to go along with the crime, but I will act so strangely that my nerdy co-worker will figure out my plight, confess his longstanding romantic interest in me, and help me foil the plot before I get into serious legal trouble.

In TV-Movie Land, "in love" equals "stupid." Women are so starved for a relationship we will suspend all common sense at the first inkling of masculine attention. And if that attention is coming from a man who appears to be everything we have ever wanted in a mate, we can be sure he's a scurrilous cad who's up to no good. Because, in TV-Movie Land, the only good guys are the "safe" guys: the cop on the case, the faithful ex who never quite got over us, or the good-natured neighbor we never even glanced at in the elevator. Shame on us for not noticing them in the first place.

It is only when our own "unrealistic" romantic aspirations take us down the wrong path that we come to our senses, shut up, and settle for the "good guy" rather than the "exciting guy."

Given this level of gullibility, is it any wonder single women are not to be trusted in airports?

Better safe than sorry.

Chapter Twenty-three

Heroine Chic

One night, not too long ago, three of my friends and I visited a trendy new restaurant a few blocks from my apartment. It was one of those really great late-summer evenings we see too rarely in New England—not too hot, with a nice breeze—so we decided to squeeze ourselves around one of the tiny café tables on the front patio to make the most of the nice weather.

At the table next to us sat two slightly-above-middle-aged women, one blonde with a great dye job and one brunette with a very bad one. They were obviously suburbanites grabbing a quick supper after an exhausting shopping spree, as was evidenced by the Chanel, Gucci, and St. John shopping bags littering the ground at their feet. We'd just gotten our first round of designer martinis when one of the women noticed us, leaned over, smiled brilliantly at me, and burbled, "I just have to tell you—you four girls look like you just stepped out of *Sex and the City*!"

She turned back to her companion, obviously impressed with her own pop culture savvy, and thus missed my silent howl of blind dismay.

This is what my life has been reduced to? I'm just a man-hungry cardboard cutout in Jimmy Choo stilettos? And this is supposed to be a *compliment?*

I suppose I should have been grateful. I mean, it's not like there's an abundance of female TV heroines I *would* be happy to be compared to.

With the exception of *Sex and the City*, if I wanted to be a female character of the nonvixen persuasion on a television series today, I'd have one of three choices:

1. I could be the smart, beautiful, impossibly skinny wife of a stone-dumb blue-collar schlub with whom I have spawned a hateful brood of precocious brats who aren't nearly as cute as everyone else thinks they are.

2. I could be a high-powered, successful single (fill in the blank). On second thought, don't bother filling in the blank, because the nature of my profession is actually irrelevant, since the entire show will revolve, not around my career, but around my disgraceful mess of a personal life . . .

3. Unless I am a doctor, a police detective, or a district attorney, in which case I will have no personal life. Except if I am also (a) a single mother, in which case that will be all anyone else will hear about; (b) having an affair with a married or womanizing co-worker, which will inevitably end in heartbreak and a suicide attempt (for me, not for him); or (c) the victim of some sort of violent crime, the brutality of which will be directly proportional to my character's strength and independence.

Sometimes they'll liven things up with a little alcoholism, a breast cancer scare, or an unplanned pregnancy that either turns out to be a false alarm resulting from a wacky mixup in the hospital lab or awakens in me a new sense of maternal responsibility heretofore unimagined, but that's pretty much the range of story options open to today's typical TV heroine.

Just once, I'd like to turn on the TV and see a show that features a normal single woman with a normal job and a normal dating life who just happens to have something interesting happen to her during the course of her ordinary day. You know, like 99.9 percent of the single women in this country.

Instead, they gave us *Sex and the City* and told us that *that* was the best representation we could hope for.

Oh, I held high hopes for this series when it debuted (and, in the ultimate exercise of masochistic hypocrisy, I watched it to the bitter end). But here's a piece of advice from someone who knows a little something about television addiction: *Never* become an early adopter of a TV show, because you always end up angry and frustrated over how it gets ruined as soon as it becomes popular. And never, under any circumstance, become an early adopter of a TV show you sort-of-kind-of identify with, because the moment they ruin that show they ruin *you* along with it.

So it was with *Sex and the City*. The most pernicious bait-and-switch in television history.

What happens when you take a fresh, funny, and, yes, sort-of-kind-of relevant look at the lives and loves of a quartet of closely knit single women (I think at one point it was even characterized as a "celebration" of singlehood) and try to make it accessible to the slurping troglodytes who are now the arbiters of what goes on American television? You end up with a half-assed morality play that's done more damage to single women than the Miss Universe Pageant and the Victoria's Secret Fashion Show combined.

> Sexually active women are not to be taken seriously. They are to be mocked, humiliated, and punished with life-threatening diseases until they come to their senses. This, we are told, is "growth" in a character.

If you watched the show from beginning to end, you can actually chart this transformation from season to season, beginning with the gradual neutering of Samantha Jones. When the show first aired, she was an independent, successful, sexually aggressive woman who loathed sentimentality and was thoroughly satisfied with her life. Flash-forward a few seasons and she turned into a cartoon character—getting squirted in the face when she tried to milk a cow, screaming and tumbling into a pile of garbage when a date took her hand, even being pelted with *linguine alla pesto* when lunching (alone, of course) in a nice restaurant. She couldn't even manage to sign for a FedEx without taking the delivery guy into the back room for a quickie. And in the final season, in exchange for this sort of ritual humiliation, the writers stuck Samantha with the old standby breast cancer storyline and left her weeping with loneliness over a bout of unsatisfying nostalgia sex with a former flame before belatedly discovering the joys of monogamy. The lesson? Sexually active women are not to be taken seriously. They are to be mocked, humiliated, and punished with life-threatening diseases until they come to their senses. This, we are told, is "growth" in a character.

And it isn't just sexual activity that must be punished—professional success takes its lumps as well. Witness poor Miranda Hobbes. A wealthy, well-educated, successful lawyer, Miranda finally made partner at her firm—something she had been working toward for years—when, right on schedule, she fell victim to that handy smack 'em down plot device designed to cow the most high-achieving ballbreaker: the Unplanned Pregnancy. So what does she do? Does she head to the clinic, have an abortion, and then go back to work, relieved the whole mess is over with? Well, what do you think? She goes to the clinic, all right, but that's only to heighten the dramatic climax when she does the "right thing" and changes her mind at the last minute! And, along with the baby, another stereotypical single TV mom is born. Because women who have sex on television are bad and must therefore suffer the screaming, drooling consequences of their actions.

Of course, the show's biggest slap in the face to the audience that made it a hit was the series finale. After insisting for six years that "you don't need a man to be happy!" the writers turned around and made certain that *every single main character*—even the Reformed Slut Samantha—ended up paired off and settled down in a long-term monogamous relationship.

Now *there's* some positive reinforcement for all you single gals out there. Single is fabulous! Except when it's, you know, *not*.

Single is fabulous! Except when it's, you know, *not*.

I really thought we'd gotten beyond this by now.

I could buy maybe one or two characters ending up as

half of a happy couple. I could even stomach three of them being paired off in the end. But *all four?* In whose world does *that* happen?

Far more troubling than simply the fact that the show paired them all off was the sacrifice it extracted from each of the main characters in order to give her that "happy ending" the ketchupy voice of Troglodyte America was clamoring for. From its inception, the show claimed to be about *not* compromising one's ideals to land a man. But by the end, Our Fearless Heroines weren't merely compromising—they were *scrambling* to renounce the most integral elements of their own identities for the sake of what were, in all honesty, some pretty sketchy relationships:

After six years of back-and-forth and some incremental steps toward self-respect, Carrie chucks it all and scurries back to "Mr. Big," a self-absorbed adulterer who had treated her like crap for six years and no doubt will continue to do so despite his protestations of love and personal growth.

Miranda torpedoes her career, hops on the Mommy Track, gives up her beloved Manhattan apartment, and moves to Brooklyn with a self-described "nice guy" who immediately foists onto her the brunt of the familial responsibility (including the care and bathing of her dementia-addled mother-in-law).

Samantha, scared straight by her brush with death, happily relinquishes her sexual independence and ends up with a handsome-but-passive mimbo* who is all too

---

* Male bimbo.

happy to let her use her previously in-demand PR skills to manage his career.

And Charlotte—poor Charlotte—gives up her religion (and, by extension, her lifelong WASP identity) and converts to Judaism to acquiesce to the selfish whim of a man who, although not particularly religious himself, refused to marry her *unless* she converted.

I suppose you could argue that all relationships are ultimately about compromise, but, silly me, I always thought compromise was a two-way kind of thing. There's no mutuality here (unless, in the case of Mr. Big, you count "putting up with Carrie's whining" as his contribution to the success of the relationship). The men all reap the benefits while the women congratulate themselves—and one another—on "maturing" and "growing" enough to not mind that they're the ones turning themselves inside out for the sake of being part of a couple. This, apparently, was more important to them than remaining true to their own selves, and the message the show sent was that this was the "happy ending" all women should aspire to. It was the "ultimate exercise of feminine independence" and a "triumph of choice," we were told.

How ironic, then, that the ultimate exercise of that independence was to sacrifice it entirely. All for the sake of some dubious companionship, a wardrobe full of overpriced shoes, and a few dozen back issues of *Vogue* with which to console themselves. That's the fairy-tale ending we have to look forward to. Thanks, *Sex and the City*.

Somehow, that's not something I see myself doing anytime soon. And, sitting on that restaurant patio that summer evening and looking across the table at my three friends, I didn't see them doing something like that, either.

We stayed at the restaurant well past dark. Long after the dinner crowd cleared out and the pedestrian traffic on the sidewalk dwindled to a trickle, and long after the ladies at the next table paid their check and asked the waiter to have the parking valet bring their car around to the front.

My friends and I watched them as they prepared to leave. They lingered for quite a while, sipping their watered-down Cosmopolitans, chatting about all the new shoes they'd bought that day, and bemoaning their husbands' inability to appreciate the urban dining experience. When they finally stood up they took great care collecting their belongings, gathering their designer shopping bags from the ground and checking beneath the table to make sure they hadn't missed anything.

Then they walked over to the front of the restaurant, loaded the bags into the back of their Chevy Suburban, climbed in, and drove away.

Slowly. Very, very slowly.

Chapter Twenty-four

Controlled Chaos

The last time we saw my poor friend "K," she was prostrate on my living room sofa, sobbing her mascara off over her latest romantic misadventure.

You'll all be relieved to know that she did manage to pick herself up from my couch, go home, and move on with her life. And you'll all be equally disgusted to learn that, when Mr. Ex materialized on her doorstep right on schedule three months later and begged for one more chance, K let him in—and ended up back in my living room, sobbing, in slightly less than forty-eight hours, undoubtedly a new world's record for the boomerang blowoff.

Some people never learn.

But K did, and she bounced back with a vengeance. Literally. One week later, seemingly recuperated from her heartbreak, she invited me out to dinner, ostensibly to thank me for the sofa-and-sympathy treatment, but really to float her latest brainstorm by me: a nationwide sex strike.

According to K, who had adopted a frightening new air of intensity around everything she did, sex is the root of all conflict between men and women. They want it. We have it. And if only all single women band together and agree to withhold it until we are all safely married, men will behave more responsibly, women will maintain their self respect, and the world will be a happier place for married and single folk alike.

"Well? What do you think?" she demanded, leaning forward a little too eagerly as she awaited my pronouncement.

I looked upon her with tender pity. "Hon," I replied, as gently as I could, "where's the upside?"

"What do you mean?"

"In the first place, you realize this means you'll be doing without sex for quite some time."

"That's okay. I don't really like it that much anyway."

"Other women might beg to differ. But that's beside the point. Let's say your little scheme works. Let's say you get your wish, the boys get desperate, and before you know it, we're all living in McMansions in the depths of suburbia with a husband, three kids, and a minivan. *Where's the upside?*"

"What are you talking about?"

"What you're saying, essentially, is that all men are dogs and they won't marry you if they don't respect you, and they won't respect you if you sleep with them. Right?"

"Right."

"They only respond to challenges and ultimatums, so if you give in too soon they'll either get bored and move on or they'll treat you like crap because they'll think you're a slut. Right?"

"Right."

"Is that the kind of person you want to be with?"

"Huh?"

"Do you really want to date a man who is so shallow and superficial he'd dump you simply because you had sex with him before he felt like you should?"

"Why not? You dumped someone because he ordered dessert for you on your first date!"

"*That's not the whole story and you know it!* Answer my question."

K didn't answer. Instead, she began to deflate visibly, her bold vision in tatters. It made me feel kind of sad, but I was on a roll.

"And another thing," I continued. "Suppose you *don't* have sex with him and you somehow manage to get him to propose to you and you end up married to him. Guess what? He's still the same shallow jerk who would have dumped you if you had slept with him way back when— except now you're stuck with him *for the rest of your life!* Who wants *that*?" I made a face and shuddered dramatically.

We finished our meal in silence, K stabbing at her salmon salad with furious indignation, and parted ways shortly thereafter. I haven't heard much from her since, but I know she'll come around to my way of thinking. Eventually.

In the meantime, I wrote her idea off as the delusional ranting of a justifiably bitter friend. Yet there was no writing off her underlying premise: In her view, women are the gatekeepers of the male sexual experience, and, as such, are expected to control male behavior through the judicious doling out of sexual favors. And, really, when you think about it, how does that differ from the underlying premise of every book, advice column, TV talk show, magazine article, and Web site that deals with love and re-lationships? In the end, isn't it all really about controlling male behavior to achieve our own ends?

> **We, the women of the world, are expected to instruct and guide the men in our lives the same way we are expected to nurture and care for their children.**

Men cannot commit—we must read self-help books written by ignorant quacks to learn how to trick them into it.

Men cannot dress themselves—we must hire a squad of handsome homosexuals to descend on their homes and re-make them in their image.

Men cannot behave in public—we must consult women's magazines to learn how to train them to use a knife and fork before they can be trusted to behave properly in a restaurant that does not have a pair of golden arches out front.

Men cannot clean—we must chuckle indulgently when they try, and then secretly follow them around with a dustpan to "fix" the disaster they create.

Men cannot decorate—we must force them to trade in their big tube television sets for smaller, lighter, more aesthetically appealing flat-screen models that blend in more seamlessly with our frilly lace curtains.

It's no wonder even they don't believe they can control themselves around women. They haven't had to think for themselves since before they were born.

Oh, yeah, and *that's* our fault, too.

We, the women of the world, are expected to instruct and guide the men in our lives the same way we are expected to nurture and care for their children. We are told that this is what we must be prepared to do to catch and keep a man. In fact, we are told, we must do this to be happy ourselves. They call it "empowerment." They tell us it is an honor.

Of course, with this great honor comes great responsibility. Inherent in our mandate is the unspoken assumption that, should we relinquish our control, we have only ourselves to blame and are thus responsible not only for the consequences of our own actions, but of theirs as well.

That's a pretty heavy burden. But refuse to accept it and be prepared: You will be branded perfectionist, uncompromising, and intractable; accused of harboring unrealistic expectations; warned about bleak lives of bitter loneliness due to your "hatred" of the opposite sex.

And no matter how many times you insist you expect more of men because you *think* more highly of them—and that you *don't* believe they're stupid, immature, sex-crazed children who must be tamed and domesticated before they can sit on the living room sofa without a strategically placed newspaper beneath them—if things go wrong, it's still your fault.

And then you have two choices. You can cry for a few days, chalk up the mistake to bad luck or bad karma, and move forward. Or, like K, you can fool yourself into believing that the right combination of trickery and manipulation will turn the tables and somehow, magically, get you the life you think you want.

Dr. John Gray and his ilk have made billions of dollars selling us on Door Number Two, because as long as we are able to blame ourselves for what goes wrong with our relationships, we can kid ourselves that changing our own behavior is the key to controlling the behavior of others. If we only master the formula, or so they would have us believe, the rest will be easy.

Of course, what they don't tell you is who's really controlling whom.

Conclusion:

Manifesto Destiny

So the question you're probably asking yourself by now is whether I actually know what I'm talking about.

The answer? Quite possibly not.

Oh, I know a lot about a lot of stuff. And I know a little about a lot more stuff. But I know absolutely nothing about a whole bunch of other stuff, which, mind you, doesn't prevent me from spouting off about it anyway. But if you think I'm trying to set myself up as the Latest Greatest Oracle of Relationship Wisdom, think again.

No matter what the experts tell you, there is no magic formula for landing a mate. And maybe that's as it should be. After all, isn't the greatest thing about love its sheer unpredictability?

Nevertheless, you've read this far—thank you!—so I assume you're looking for some sort of inspirational advice to guide you as you go about the remainder of your life. And if that's the case, you're obviously still . . . *out there.*

God love ya.

I honestly don't have the heart to dash your hopes and crush your little spirits myself—reality will take care of that soon enough. Instead, I feel it my solemn duty to support and instruct you in the ways of this callous world, because, based on all the wailing and gnashing of teeth I've heard out there, you need all the help you can get.

Thus, even though I'm the last person in the world you should be coming to for advice on how to get married, allow me to give you something that's far more important: advice on how to be single. I like to think of it as my "Singular Manifesto," a Bill of Rights, if you will, for those of you who have tired of all the chipper, happy, "buck up—it's not that bad!" bullshit you usually hear when your marital status comes into question.

So here's a dose of hard-core, in-your-face, reality-based advice that is definitely *not* intended to help you land the perfect spouse but just might prevent you from landing the wrong one.

Ready? Here goes.

❊ *The Singular Manifesto* ❊

ARTICLE 1: You have the right to be picky. Enough, already, with the whole "You're too picky and no one is ever going to live up to your unrealistic expectations" crap. Of course you're picky! You *should* be picky! You're looking for a *life partner*, not a sweater. Personally, I don't think people are picky enough. The pressure to couple up in this society is so unrelenting it's bound to break even the most confirmed bachelors and bachelorettes among us. But here's a little secret: You know all those people who are always running around complaining about how "hard" marriage is? You know why it's so hard for them? Because they never really wanted to be married in the first place! They're sharing a life day in, day out, with someone they never really liked all that much to begin with but shrugged and settled for because they were tired of all the nagging! That's why so few widows end up remarrying after their spouses die. They've been there. They know better. So aim high—your very sanity hangs in the balance.

ARTICLE 2: You have the right to give what you get. I don't know what it is about the relationship game that makes us tolerate behavior that would be absolutely unacceptable anywhere else, but from here on out you have my express permission to reciprocate in kind whenever someone's behavior exceeds the bounds of human tolerance. The Internet date who ended up being six inches shorter, thirty years older, and a whole lot more pockmarked than the picture on his profile? That's grounds for on-the-spot termination of the evening without further comment or explanation. The same goes for blowhards who are snotty to the waitstaff, creeps who won't leave you alone in airport waiting lounges, assholes who won't get off—let alone turn off—their cell phones at the movies, and manipulative freaks who force you to consume desserts you don't want. You don't need any explanations, polite excuses, or preplanned "fallback" phone calls from friends designed to rescue you from a potentially horrible evening with any of these people. They need to be kicked to the curb rapidly, bluntly, and without further ado. How else will they learn? Repeat after me: "This isn't working out. I don't like you. I'm going home." These magic words will extricate you from any bad social situation with no need for elaboration. Use them. Use them a lot. They will work. And if they don't—well, then, that just proves my point, doesn't it?

ARTICLE 3: You have the right to tell well-meaning friends and relatives to bugger off when they begin to pester you about your marital status. Why do people feel so entitled to meddle in one of the most personal decisions you will ever make? They're not and they shouldn't, but the only way they're ever going to learn this is if you tell them so. And this applies particularly to those well-meaning friends and relatives who have a track record of setting you up on blind dates with losers. You are not obliged to suffer through yet another evening of dull conversations and awkward silences simply because your Aunt Ethel's next door neighbor's cousin's brother-in-law just got divorced for the third time and is "actively looking." In the words of Nancy Reagan: Just Say No. It feels good. Trust me.

ARTICLE 4: You have the right to completely screw up your love life and get upset about it anyway. The phrases "It's my own fault," "I should have known better," and "I was so stupid" are to be permanently excised from the Singular Vernacular. Maybe it was, maybe you should have, and maybe you were—but so what? If someone is treating you badly, it's that person's fault, not yours. You're the victim here, so act like it! Snarl, storm around, rant away to your friends, plot revenge, and feel as bitter and betrayed as you like. Your love is a very precious, special, and unique gift. It is not given freely, and when it *is* given it deserves to be taken seriously. And when it is not taken seriously, when someone else stomps on it thought-lessly and callously, you have the right to be outraged. Period. How dare they?

ARTICLE 5: You have the right to hope. You are not stupid or naive to want to believe the best about the people you love. You are not a fool for telling yourself that someone has not called you back because he or she is "too busy at work." You are not an idiot because you have an ideal and refuse to compromise on that ideal simply because everyone else tells you you're crazy. You are only wrong if you let your hope take over your life and inform every decision you make, blinding you to reality and paralyzing your future. That's when I might have to show up at your door and shake a little sense into you.

The late, great Ann Landers once wrote, "It's better to be alone than to wish you were." There is nothing lonelier than being trapped inside a life with someone you don't want to be with. It's like being on a bad date that never ends. Believe me—that will break your spirit a lot more quickly than even the most singular of existences.

And, deep down, you know this. That's why you picked this book up in the first place. Because *you know*.

You know ending up single is not the worst thing that can happen to you.

It might even be . . . dare I say it?

A blessing in the skies.

...And Another Thing:

Author Notes on Singular Existence

Singular Existence actually began as a letter to the editor of the *Boston Globe* in response to its article about the Michigan State University study claiming single people who live alone are endangering the environment. Yes, there was a real study, and, yes, they really did write an article about it. All true. In fact, pretty much everything in the book is true. I've changed some names (and left others intact—you people all know who you are, and if you don't, it's because I don't want you to) and altered some facts here and there to keep from pissing off some of my subjects, but, on the "truthiness" (thank you, Stephen Colbert) scale, *Singular Existence* scores about 95 out of 100. So suck on a million little pieces of *that*, James Frey.

At any rate, the *Globe* article made me mad. And, when I get mad, my first inclination is to sit down and fire off a withering e-mail to whomever has offended me, which I usually either save to draft or delete entirely when I realize sending said withering e-mail will result in the loss of either (a) my job; (b) my friends; or (c) my liberty if the National Security Agency were to get its hands on my e-mail account. In this case, however, I actually liked what I had to say. The problem was, the "object" of my wrath turned out to be not so much one reporter's silly little twist on what was probably a quite serious academic study, but the overarching notion that being single in our society is considered so unquestioningly "bad" that these types of articles slip by editorial boards every single day with nary a blink or eye roll.

That, and the fact that my letter was more than five pages long, and more than a tad snarky, which rendered it completely unpublishable in a mainstream newspaper.

Rather than simply chuck the idea of responding to the article, however, I toyed with the idea of using it to jump-start my years-old novel, and even wrote several pages along that line. But something odd happened as I neared completion of my tenth page. I realized that what I had written was 90 percent opinion and only 10 percent fiction. So, rather than go back and try to reconfigure it into something more novel-esque, I decided to ditch the novel entirely and just go with what I had. And, once I made that decision, I discovered that, well, I had a heck of a lot to say about the state of singlehood today. More than a letter to the editor, the occasional op-ed, or even a humorous novel could possibly convey.

And *Singular Existence* was born.

My goal in writing this book was to give single people—women *and* men—something different to read about themselves. God knows, there are more books for single people on the shelves today than there are single people to read them. But most nonfiction books targeting my demographic, even the funny ones, tend to fall into three categories:

1. Well-worn rants lamenting the miserable indignity of singlehood: "Why do older men get to date younger women, but older women end up alone—*wahhh!*" "Why are there so many great single women out there but no eligible men—*boo-hooo!*"

2. Faux "self-help" tomes that list in vicious, accusatory detail everything women are doing wrong in relationships: "It's *your* fault you're single because you're too (choose one): **FAT, UGLY, STUPID, EDUCATED, SUCCESSFUL, PICKY, ASSERTIVE, NEEDY, ALL OF THE ABOVE**.

3. The so-called "Celebrate Your Singlehood!" genre, which offers relentlessly cheerful, upbeat advice for overcoming the crushing loneliness in store for us for the rest of our lives: "Have a candlelight dinner for yourself!" "Share some ice cream with your cat!" "Here are ten financial strategies to ensure that even though you're going to die alone, at least you'll die rich!"

I didn't want to write one of those books. I didn't want to write something that defined single people by some perceived deficiency in our lives or presented singlehood as a liability to be overcome. Instead, I wanted to confront the mind-set that assumes that deficiency and assigns that liability in the first place. How can you stay true to yourself and maintain your own unique identity—safeguard your *singular existence*, if you will—in the face of society's relentless pursuit of coupledom at all costs?

I guess it's up to you to determine how close I've come to accomplishing this goal.

Thanks for reading!

Talk Amongst Yourselves:

A Discussion Guide for Singular Existence

I was never a very dutiful book club participant. I've belonged to one or two in my day, but, to be honest, I really only went for the free wine and cheese and was always more of the, "What do you mean I had to READ something for this?" mind-set when it came down to the actual discussion portion of the get-together.

This was partially due to the fact that I tend to prefer nonfiction to fiction. Fiction is fun to listen to in the car on long trips, and there is definitely something to be said for curling up in a big chair with a really great novel and a full glass of red wine on a rainy Sunday afternoon. But, all in all, if I'm going to read a book rather than, say, go to the movies or watch TV, I like to think I'm learning a little something about the world in the process. It's my little way of multitasking.

Unfortunately, the book clubs I've been invited to join have tended to focus more on fiction. "Literary" fiction, that is. As in the *Memoirs of a Geisha, Life of Pi, Kite Runner* kind of fiction. And—at the risk of co-opting the world's most obnoxious catch phrase—*I'm just not into that*. Nothing wrong with good literary fiction—hell, I wish I could write it. But my literary tastes tend to be of the more mass-market, Neanderthal variety: serial killers, ethically challenged attorneys, daring epidemiologists tracking sudden outbreaks of flesh-eating plague viruses. That's my bag. Not exactly the stuff of scintillating book club conversations, if you know what I mean.

Given all the above, I'm quite flattered you've all busted the paradigm and selected my modest little nonfiction essay collection for this week's reading assignment. I hope you enjoyed reading it, and I wish I could be there to thank you in person for all the nice things you are undoubtedly saying about it to your fellow members at this very moment. Since I can't be there, however, I would like to give you the next best thing: a little context for your discussion. Just picture me up on a big video screen looking down upon you, Big Brother–ish, adding my two cents here and there as you talk amongst yourselves about, well, *me*.

So—let's get cracking, shall we?

❖ *Part One* ❖

Hopelessly (Out)Dated

This section deals with the relentless pressure imposed on single people to just "get out there and *date*, dammit!" Not only does this pressure affect the way we relate to one another, it also affects the way we view ourselves. Think about your own attitude toward dating and relationships and ask yourself how your thinking has changed over time based on external forces—be it friends, family, or society in general:

1. *Fully Uncommitted:* Does "commitmentphobia" really exist, or is it one of those made-up syndromes designed to sell advice books to the broken-hearted? And if it's not a real psychiatric disorder, what do you think really lies behind some people's reluctance to commit?

2. *Just Desserts:* Are women's expectations and aspirations *really* that unreasonable when it comes to choosing a life partner? What is it we *want*, anyway? And how far are you willing to compromise for the sake of a relationship?

3. *The Rules of Disengagement:* Here's one you can have fun with: Share your worst breakup stories—your own or your friends' (urban legends encouraged). What's your personal code of ethics when it comes to breaking up?

4. *Shallow, Self-Centered, and Opinionated Seeks Opposite:* There are entire businesses out there devoted to helping people write and market themselves in personal ads. What would make you (or has made you) respond to someone's personal ad, and what would send you screaming into the night?

5. *Share and Share Alone:* When does casual conversation cross the line into oversharing? What subjects do you consider off limits on a first or second date? Where do you fall on the "sharing" meter?

6. *It's Not the Heat . . . It's the Hostility:* Why the heck are we all so angry about dating, anyway? Is it simply the fear of rejection, or is there something more

there? Have you ever encountered outright hostility in a dating situation?

7. *Blessings in the Sky:* Think back to your last serious relationship and ask yourself whether there might, in fact, be worse fates than ending up single. What, ultimately, split you up? Where would you be today if things had "worked out" for you and your ex?

✳ *Part Two* ✳

Married by the Mob

I like to think of this section as the "careful what you wish for, folks" part of the book. We've all grown up with a very idealized vision of what marriage is supposed to be, beginning with the little-girl dream of the "perfect wedding." But, as many people realize a little too late, reality is often at odds with this dream. So then what?

8. *Never a Bridesmaid:* What do your married friends say about marriage now versus what they might have said before their wedding?

9. *Warning—Contents May Settle:* Everyone has at least one friend who married someone who's kind of a, well, *tool*. Assuming that this friend is not a member of your book club, *spill*. Why do you think she settled, and do you think she knew it at the time?

10. *Get Her to the Church in Time:* Who Wants to Marry My Daughter—tacky display of vulgar desperation, or nifty solution to the welfare crisis? Discuss!

11. *Deconstructing the Married Guy:* What makes the Married Guy tick? How would you react if you found out your husband was crawling through trendy bars hitting on attractive single women? When does harmless flirtation cross the line into something more insidious?

12. *I Don't Know Why She Does It:* For a society that claims to venerate mothers, we certainly send mixed messages to both working and stay-at-home mothers. Is this what's behind the so-called Mommy Wars? Do some women defend their motherhood decisions so aggressively because they feel no one else will?

13–14. *I Kid You Not/The Hardest Job in the World:* It seems like everywhere we turn these days we're always being admonished to *"think about the chill-drennn."* Has your own attitude toward children changed as you've grown older? For better or worse?

15. *Proprietary Values:* Same-sex marriage is a hugely controversial topic, even for people who favor gay rights in general. Where do you stand? What does your own support of or opposition to same-sex marriage reveal about your attitude toward marriage in general? Do you feel it's reasonable or unreasonable?

❊ *Part Three* ❊

A Culture of Strife

This section was originally intended to be two parts: one dealing with pop culture, and the other with society's attitude toward marriage and singlehood in general. But, as I began assigning essays to each section, I realized the two were so hopelessly intertwined they really belonged in the same category. How *does* our societal imperative to couple up and settle down inform our popular culture—and your life in particular?

16. *Mars and Venus Go to Hell:* Dr. John Gray: Well-meaning pundit, or Antichrist? How in the world did this man become so popular? Is there any truth to the idea that all our problems boil down to miscommunication, and, if so, how does it affect your own behavior in your relationships?

17. *Grating Expectations:* Why is the media so quick to hype stories that discourage women from pursuing professional or academic success? What do we have to fear? And who benefits when we temper our expectations?

18. *He's Just a Big Fat Asshole:* Why do so many people gravitate to the "blame the victim" school of thought when it comes to self-help books? What do you think this attitude reveals about the authors' opinions of their readers? Does blaming yourself for a failed relationship make you feel better or

worse in the long run? How does it affect the way you approach future relationships?

19. *A Manly Pursuit:* What's your personal definition of "manliness"? Does it differ significantly from, say, the Dodge Motors definition? In what way?

20. *Read It and Weep:* Does Chick Lit send the message that professional success is meaningless without a husband or boyfriend to share it with? Are there any books out there deemed Chick Lit that show exceptions to this rule? What makes them different?

21. *Remote Acceptability:* How do you feel about the notion that it's up to women to "civilize" the savage male of the species? Are you up to the task? And what does it say about our society's image of men?

22. *Profiles in Scurrilage:* Such shows as *Sex and the City, Alias*, and the like purport to portray single women as strong, confident, and intelligent. Yet there's often an undercurrent of sadness, loneliness, or desperation (or, as network executives call it, "vulnerability") driving even the toughest TV heroines. Why do you think this is? Does it work for us or against us in the long run?

23. *Heroine Chic:* Why do so many books and television shows that supposedly "celebrate" the idea of singlehood eventually yank the rug out from beneath their fans by pairing off the heroine? Are we all really looking for that "fairy-tale" ending?

24. *Controlled Chaos:* Is it really all just about sex in the end? Do you think men and women really have

such different priorities when it comes to relationships? How does our presumed "gatekeeper" function both inhibit and protect us from emotional pain?

Manifesto Destiny: If there were one thing you could change about society's view of single people, what would it be? And how would this change impact the way you live your life as a unique, relevant individual who—married or single—makes a difference on our planet?

Whew. That's a lot to talk about in a single evening. I hope you had plenty of wine and cheese on hand. I had no idea I was so deep!

Maybe there's hope for me as an author of literary fiction after all.

Acknowledgments

*(aka "Please God Don't Let Me
Forget Anyone")*

I've often wondered why so many authors thank their agents and editors ahead of everyone else, including those who have given birth and supported said authors their entire lives. Now that I know Elisabeth Weed and Danielle Chiotti, I completely understand. From the moment I met Elisabeth, I knew she was the perfect agent for me—which she proved immediately by finding, in Danielle, the perfect editor. Not only did both these incredible women "get" what I was trying to say, they were both brave enough to take a tremendous leap of faith on a first-time author and, in doing so, enabled me to finally create the book that had been inside me all my life.

Of course, that doesn't mean I shouldn't also thank my family, beginning with my parents, whose patience, understanding, and support know no bounds; as well as my sisters and best friends, Liz and Leigh, for their love, encouragement, and unwavering faith in me.

In addition, I owe a tremendous debt to my mentor, business partner, and dear friend Kristin Lund, who, by proving to me that "of course" I could be a writer, quite literally changed my life forever.

Thanks also to my fellow "Splinters": R. J. Bardsley, Chuck Leddy, Randy Meyers, Paul Parcellin, Jill Rubinstein, Len Sparks, and Kate Wilkinson, whose constant encouragement and not-so-gentle prodding finally convinced me it was time to send my little book out into the world.

In addition, thank you to those of you who helped make *Singular Existence* a reality: Jessie Reed, for encouraging me to start my site, and Cathy, Owen, and Charlotte Jacobs for inspiring me to keep it going; my one-woman press agent Kathy Parker for continuing to bring in the readers; my good friends Ted Lund, Norah Hass, Scott Benjamin, Charlie and Karen Korn, Cheryl Bliss, Anisha Mason, and the lovely Nancy Willoughby for cheering me on; Claire Folger, Kathy Stauner, and Chris Smith for helping me overcome the trauma of the dreaded "author photo"; Chris Castellani, the gang at Grub Street, and the bloggers at Salon.com for welcoming me so warmly and unquestioningly into their communities; and Kristen Hayes and the entire staff at Citadel for making *Singular Existence* look as much fun as it was to write.

Last but not least, I want to thank my ever-patient and faithful readers whose comments, feedback, and dedication have helped me become a better writer, if not a better person.

Okay, definitely not a better person. But thanks for trying.